SONG OF THE SKY

SONG OF THE SKY

Versions of Native American Song-Poems
by BRIAN SWANN

REVISED AND EXPANDED EDITION

FOREWORD BY BARRY O'CONNELL

The University of Massachusetts Press   Amherst

Published 1985 by Four Zoas Night House, Ltd.
Revised edition published 1993 by
The University of Massachusetts Press

LC 93–5152
ISBN 0–87023–872–8
Library of Congress Cataloging-in-Publication Data

Swann, Brian.
Song of the sky : versions of Native American songs-poems / by
Brian Swann; foreword by Barry O'Connell. —Rev. ed.
p.   cm.
Includes bibliographical references.
ISBN 0–87023–872–8 (alk. : pprbck.)
1. Indians of North America—Songs and music—Adaptations.
2. Indians of North America—Poetry 3. Indian poetry—Adaptations.
I. Title.
PS3569.W256S66 1993
811'.53—dc20   93–5152
                                                                             CIP
British Library Cataloguing in Publication data are available.

The three woodcuts by Julia Ferrari are based on Native American pottery motifs found in
Authentic Indian Designs: 2500 Illustrations from Reports of the Bureau of American Ethnology, ed.
Maria Naylor (New York: Dover Publications, 1975). Other pottery motifs from the same
source have been used throughout this volume.

TABLE OF CONTENTS

Adaptations for the revised edition from the work of

EARLIEST RECORDED MUSIC

Ni-na ha-ni, ni-na ha-ni, ni-na ha-ni, na-ni

on-go. Ni-na ha-ni, ni-na ha-ni, ni-na ha-ni,

ho-ho, ni-na ha-ni, ni-na ha-ni, ni-na ha-ni,

Ca-ous-ban-no-gue at-chit-cha co-gue a-que a-ona

ba-no-gue a-chit-cha scha-go-be he he he.

Mintin-go-mi ta-de pi-ni pi-ni he a-chit-cha.-le

matchi-minam-ba, mic-tande mic-tan-de pi-ni pini he.

The music reproduced above is the first Indian music recorded in North America. Father Marquette, on his First Voyage (1674), provided the words of an Illinois song, but no music. The Illinois, he said, give the song "a certain turn which cannot be sufficiently expressed by note, but which nevertheless constitutes all its grace." The words Marquette provided are: "Ninahani, ninahani, ninahani, nani ongo." The music for this calumet dance was found later in a manuscript preserved by the Jesuits in Paris. (*The Indians of North America*, selected and edited by Edna Kenton, volume 2, New York 1927, p. 274 and pp. 551-552. This book consists of excerpts from Thwaites' *Jesuit Relations*.)

PREFACE TO THE REVISED EDITION

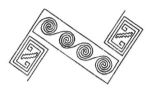

The original *Song of the Sky* was published by Dan Carr and Julia Ferrari's Four Zoas Night House in 1985. This handsome edition went out of print in 1989. In 1992, Arnold Krupat introduced me to Barry O'Connell, whose exemplary *On Our Own Ground: The Complete Writings of William Apess, a Pequot*, had just been published by the University of Massachusetts Press. O'Connell thought that the press might be interested in reviving *Song of the Sky*, and he volunteered to make the contacts. When Massachusetts agreed to be the publisher, O'Connell kindly wrote the new Foreword. I am most grateful to him, and to Clark Dougan, senior editor, as well as to Bruce Wilcox, director.

I thought of up-dating, making changes in the Introduction and Notes for this new edition, but in the end, apart from correcting some errors, I decided to keep those sections largely as they were. I would, however, like to touch here on a remark I made in the first note of the Introduction. I said that Dell Hymes' call for translations using "anthropological philology" had not been followed "to any great degree." The last decade, however, has witnessed a tremendous flowering of such "ethnopoetic" translations, a fact best seen by looking at *Coming to Light: Contemporary Translations of the Native Literature of North America*, which I edited and which Random House will publish in 1994. It can also be seen in the essays and translations found in *On the Translation of Native American Literatures*, which I edited and which The Smithsonian Institution Press published in 1992.

I would like to reiterate what I have said from the beginning: These poems are *not* translations. *On the Translation of Native American Literatures* and *Coming to Light* will show the reader what translations are, or can be. Yet if these poems are not translations they are also not (as one reviewer claimed) simply "poems in their own right"; they are not entirely "self sufficient." They may still be "only white man's poetry," but they have gone through a series of mediations and filters to exist somewhere between the individual lyric voice and cultures that are not mine.

In the decade or so since I began this book, I have continued to look out for songs that lend themselves to my approach. (Most, of course, do not. Many are wordless, ranging from pure 'vocables' to the 'sobbing' songs of northwest California or the 'true crying' of personal medicine songs and most of the Ghost Dance songs where 'texts' are cryptic descriptions of visions, fully understood only by the inventors.) I have found a number and have added them in a separate section following the earlier adaptations, which are all unchanged.

INTRODUCTION

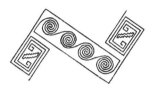

What I have attempted in these versions is to bring over that small part of the originals which is accessible to me. They are what Thoreau would have called "only white man's poetry." Anything else would have been presumptuous if not impossible.[1] For, as Paula Gunn Allen has pointed out in her essay "The Sacred Hoop" (in Abraham Chapman, ed., *Literature of the American Indians*, New York, 1975), Native American literature and Western literature are hardly compatible. Basic assumptions about the universe are not the same. The purpose of Native American literature (songs, ceremonies, legends, myths) is to "embody, articulate and share reality, and bring the isolated private self into harmony and balance with this reality."[2]

Many of these songs or poems exist at the center of their culture. They occupy, as Kenneth Rexroth has pointed out, "a position somewhat like the sacraments and sacramentals of the so-called higher religions. . . . Poetry or song does not only play a vatic role in the society, but is itself a numinous thing."[3] Moreover, in his study of the ethnomusicology of the Flathead Indians, Alan P. Merriam notes something which applies to many other Indian groups, namely that "the single most important fact about music and its relationship to the total world is its origin in the supernatural sphere."[4] While some songs are composed by individuals, and others are borrowed from neighboring peoples, "all true and proper songs," especially in the past, originate in contacts with supernatural beings, often in the dream vision experience. These songs confer power and skills; in fact they hold society together. No one can be considered successful until he has acquired his song. The attitude of the Flathead to songs is not aesthetic. There is no psychic distance between individual and song. There is no 'art'. "The Flathead," writes Merriam, "do not conceive of their songs as entities to be taken out of context and examined as if they were objects in themselves" (p. 44). Songs are part of "the total world." (David P. McAllester makes the same point in his "Enemy Way Music: A Study of Social and Aesthetic Values as Seen in Navajo Music," *Papers of the Peabody Museum of American Archeology and Ethnology*, vol. XLI, no.3, 1954.)

The mere translation of words cannot convey much of the impact of the original occasion. In our culture, words have been separated from a whole sense of being. Too often, they are only "a temporary stay against confusion." We no longer believe in them while we use them. Poets, to be sure, retain some of the ancient respect for words as mythic entelechy, when transformation creates reciprocity and respect. But in Native American society this seems to be pervasive and not limited to one small and easily ignored group of people. In an article in *Sun Tracks*, Spring 1977, Simon Ortiz says that a hunting song, for example, is expression and perception, an active relationship with the hunting act: "The purpose of the song is first of all to do things well, the way that they're supposed to be done, part of it being the singing and performing of the song. And that I receive, again well and properly, the things that are meant to be returned to me. I express myself as well as realize the experience." The song is experiential. There is an intimate connection between right acting and right singing. Everything is reciprocal. Everything is alive.

In Native American cultures there are love songs, war songs, songs sung in stories, game songs, lullabies (except, according to Densmore, among the Cheyenne),[5] and other secular songs, or what the Flathead call "make-up songs," songs with no inherent power. (In former times it was believed that all songs were 'sacred'. There were no "make-up songs.")[6] There are also songs which form part of large sacred ceremonies. And there are songs of healing, when the singer is implicated in his or her song in ways foreign to us. His inspiration takes him outside self and inside other; he mediates between ordinary and separate reality. He sings for results. He attempts to make things happen. The song is serious; it is not sung to pass the time. Sometimes, instead of ordinary words, the singer will use archaic terms, or even a foreign language. At other times, he may use so-called 'nonsense' syllables (see later in this Introduction, and note 19). Dennis and Barbara Tedlock suggest that these nonsense syllable ("or better, abstract syllables")[7] together with the archaic terms and foreign languages, link the singer to the visionary experience. All three share in an *otherness*.[8] In addition, they note that "This is a noncalculative use of language, a way of communicating directly the joy and strangeness of the other world without explaining it away in ordinary language."[9] The singer/poet/shaman, moreover, is suffused with divine afflatus. He is the archetypal poet figure, common to most cultures at one time or another. His song is one of the roots of lyric, to use Andrew Welsh's phrase.[10]

These poems of mine are *not* translations. A new and exciting way of translation is being developed by a number of scholars and scholar-poets, starting with Dell Hymes and Dennis Tedlock.[11] We are being made aware of what might be called oral literary techniques and devices; a deep, not a glossed structure. It has taken many years for collectors and scholars to discover and acknowledge that Indians had any real kind of organizing principles in their verbal and musical art. To the early settlers, Indian songs were no better than terrifying animal howls, and even those who 'favored' the Indian in the nineteenth century found the songs to be "the wild yells of the uncivilized."[12] Only with the early twentieth century does the idea develop that Indian songs have their own principles of organization. Helen H. Roberts wrote in 1924: "The only way in which these points of structure and interpretation may be definitely determined is by putting the questions to the singers themselves and discovering what are their ideas of form. That they possess such we are coming to realize more and more."[13]

My own versions are based on field-work by some people whose various assumptions about the Indian could not but color their recordings. What Roy Harvey Pearce has called "savagism" is implicit, to one degree or another, in the work of a number of these collectors. For instance, Frances Densmore was a "friend" to the Indian in the traditional way. She believed he was a "savage" on the way to "development." She had definite notions about musical correctness, also. The Indian, she said, "has no ideas of true pitch." In other words, her ear was recording through a Western filter. How far such prejudice influenced her recording is hard to know. But perhaps a little skepticism is in place. Moreover, her real interest is the music, and sometimes she will only give a selection of the words to a dance or a song. (For more on Frances Densmore, see *Frances Densmore and Indian Music: A Memorial Volume*, compiled and edited by Charles Hofmann: Contributions from the Museum of the American Indian Heye Foundation, Vol. XXIII, New York, 1968.)[14]

Something along the same lines could be said of Marius Barbeau, who didn't even like the idea that the Northwest Indians were American. He found various homes for them to have strayed from, including China. The Indians, moreover, "are Asiatic-like: their faces resemble Buddha's: a mixture of self-indulgence and mysticism—broad, massive and sensuous, yet with a mysterious twinkle in the eye that is a riddle" ("Songs of the Northwest," *The Musical Quarterly*, vol. XIX, no. 4, 1933).

But it is too easy to make fun of the early collectors. The fact is, their contributions were enormous, and numbers of them did make an honest attempt to break through ingrained cultural habits. E. G. Stricklen in 1923, for example, found himself baffled by Papago key signatures. Although he suspected that the Papago were not using "any of the modes or keys of Western music," he believed that: "If we assume the existence of a feeling for scales on the part of the Indian singer, we may determine the scales upon which the songs are based."[15] Squeezing and fitting, he came up with the required scales and keys. But he had the modesty and honesty to note that the "measure-groups" were "unusual," and produced "designs in musical form which are new to us and yet give us a sense of symmetry."[16] He could see clearly the "skill that conceals,"[17] the difficulty of the songs, the art that masks art, just as Benjamin Ives Gilman, while ethnocentric, could yet break through to the insight that the "anomalies" of Indian music contain its "secret" and he could attempt to understand

5

the music on its own terms, as "a type apart" (*Hopi Songs*, Boston 1908).

In more recent years, with such skilled musicologists as Bruno Nettl, Gertrude Kurath, Alan Merriam, David McAllester, and others, sophisticated techniques of analysis and appreciation have been developed. Other approaches may be forthcoming. Perhaps the method of electronic transcription which Bruno Nettl describes may be used more widely (*Folk and Traditional Music of the Western Continents*, Englewood Cliffs, 1973, p. 33). Or perhaps work will be done along the linguistic lines suggested by Neil Leonard in his study of jazz, a study predicated upon the fact that Western musical ideas are not particularly fruitful when applied to African music.[18]

In many of these poems, I have tried to utilize the silence of space—silence plays an important part in Indian culture. I have tried to allow the shape of that space to enact a meaning. I have attempted, also, to treat the texts as live objects, and not as pelts and skeletons.

By using, much of the time, a 'concrete' approach, where shape creates tension and movement, I intended the poem to do its own dance in the shape it creates for itself. In this sense, I have added my own pennyworth to the creation of an 'oral poetics'. The air between the words is almost as important as the words themselves.

"A strange culture is precious," writes William Bevis in his essay "American Indian Verse Translations" (in Chapman). "Its strangeness gives us distance from ourselves." I make no pretense to being able to provide "easy entry into a strange world." The notes are there to remind us that the versions cannot stand alone. The originals cannot be transformed into simple American lyrics. I offer shadows of shadows, more than is usual in translations, more so than in translating from Italian, say, where two cultures, whatever their differences, have a broad common cultural and linguistic ground. But a common humanity should transcend most differences.

I started this project soon after coming across Natalie Curtis' *The Indians' Book* of 1907, which was the first publication to introduce the rich variety of Indian poetry to the public. I was attracted to the word-by-word translations at the end of the book, and not by her verbose rewriting of the poems. I wanted to get back some of the terseness of the 'original': I wanted stripped-down versions. Curtis' method of translation can be demonstrated from the Huma song entitled "Arawp" (admittedly an extreme example):

> 'Mai ariwa—
> 'riwa—
> 'Mai ariwa—
> 'riwa—

6

Shakwa tza mi na hi
Shakwa tza mi na

Hunya kwa pai va
Hunya kwa hui pa

This is the translation:

Song of the Mocking-Bird

Thin little clouds are spread
Across the blue of the sky,
Thin little clouds are spread—
Oh, happy am I as I sing,
I sing of the clouds in the sky.

Thus tells the bird,
'Tis the mocking-bird who sings,
And I stop to hear,
For he is glad at heart
And I will list to his message.

Then up the hill,
Up the hill I go my straight road,
The road of good—
Up the hill I go my straight road,
The happy road and good.

I have tried to cut down on words, though when necessary knowledge could be incorporated into the text, I have done so. I have also reduced repetitions, especially the 'meaningless' syllables discussed earlier, even though Inés Talamantez has called these repetitions "the very core of Native American verbal art" (M.L.A. Convention, December 1978). I simply do not understand these repetitions well enough, so I felt there was no way in which I could use them.[19]

With a number of songs I allowed myself latitude. In fact, it was often impossible not to allow oneself latitude since many of the original translations were what Francis La Flesche calls "free," and John R. Swanton notes in his introduction to his *Tlingit Myths and Texts* that many songs were "difficult to understand even in the light of the native explanation." Sometimes the informants themselves were unsure of a song's meaning. In some cases I took a stab at the meaning and called it intuition.

As for the selection process, many songs require a large apparatus to explain references to myths, ceremonies, contemporary events, social relationships. To a larger extent than when translating, say, Greek literature, we Anglos are outsiders. These songs tend to be extremely cryptic, and I had to stay clear of most of them. I do not know enough. (I recall Margot Astrov, and Ruth Underhill too, once asked why so few words are used in the songs. Because we know so much, they were told.)

From a rich variety of formal songs incorporated in ceremony, and from informal, even impromptu, songs, I have chosen songs which the Anglo reader, trained in certain attitudes, could take pleasure in and perhaps learn from (as I myself learned). I feel that this is not enough, however, and so I would strongly urge the reader to go back to the original texts, to the faint echoes of the full worlds of the tribal peoples we have done our best to extirpate;[20] worlds vital still, but terribly diminished and still under enormous pressure from a new form of genocide, from what Winona La Duke calls "genocide by energy development."[21]

One can go back to the texts, and one can avail oneself of traditional Indian hospitality by going to a pow-wow, where music is everywhere. For Indian music today is developing and flourishing, especially the music accompanying social dances. This may be due to the fact that the role of Indian music now is as a symbol of Indian identity.[22]

NOTES TO INTRODUCTION

1 Impossible for me that is. If one starts from another position better things might be forthcoming. Dennis Tedlock's work is one example of what can be done, and he writes that "we shall never develop an effective oral poetics if we begin with the structural analysis of conventional written texts" ("Toward an Oral Poetics," *New Literary History*, vol. VIII, no. 3, Spring 1977, p. 508). Dell Hymes' approach is different again. In his essay "Some North Pacific Coast Poems: A Problem in Anthropological Philology" (*American Anthropologist*, vol. 67, no. 2, April 1965, p. 335), he writes: "For the true values of the original structures and content of the poems to be realized, where now obscured, and for verbally effective translations to be newly made, the perspectives and tools of linguistics are indispensable." He also calls for the utilization of "anthropological philology." Hymes' approach has not yet been followed to any great degree, possibly because the translator would have to be a trained anthropologist, philologist, and linguist, as well as a decent poet! (For more on Hymes' approach, see the note to No. 36, *Haida Songs*.)

2 Perhaps it is not out of place here to note an important recent development in scientific thought. Are scientists discovering a truth Indians have known all along, that the world is entire and whole, indivisible, inseparable from us? Note statements such as this: "We have to cross out that old word 'observer' and replace it with the new word 'participator'. In some strange sense the quantum principle tells us that we are dealing with a participatory universe" (J. A. Wheeler, "Is Physics Legislated by Cosmogony?" in *The Encyclopedia of Ignorance,* ed. Ronald Duncan and Miranda Weston-Smith, New York, 1977, p. 30). The quantum principle joins participator with system in a "wholeness" (Niels Bohr). The universe is not 'out there', but inseparable from ourselves. A cosmic community is reinstated. And a sense of cosmic unity runs throughout the teachings of Indian medicine-men such as Lame Deer who said "the spirit is everywhere." "Power," he said, "is a two-way thing." This idea of continuity is taken up by another well-known scientist in another essay in the same book. E. W. F. Tomlin writes in "Fallacies of Evolutionary Theory," that there is no inorganic dead world. "Evolution is from the organic to the organic." We must do away "with the notion of an inorganic world." "The concept of life necessarily" requires an extension, he remarks. If the world of atom and molecule is alive, everything is alive. "The world consists of individualities of beings." News, perhaps, to dualistic Westerners, but not to mystics, and not to poets. And not to Indians. One wonders how long it will be before this truly revolutionary knowledge will seep down into our consciousness and change us. (If we prefer not to read rather abstruse scientific essays, we should listen to important 'general' writers, such as Philip Salter in *Earthwalk*. And if we'd rather read poets, there's Blake, whose vision of the universe as the Imagination is amazingly close to the view we have been describing above. "This Swedeborgian and Blakean conception of the universe rather as a person than an object strikes the modern mind as strange," notes Kathleen Raine. But she links it to other civilizations, notably Iranian mysticism. She might equally have adduced Native American consciousness. (For more, see Raine's "Science and Imagination in William Blake," *Temenos*, no. 1, 1981, 37–58.)

3 "American Indian Songs," *Assays* (New York, 1961), p. 56.

4 *Ethnomusicology of the Flathead Indians*, Viking Fund Publications in Anthropology (New York, 1967), p. 3.

5 *Cheyenne and Arapaho Music*, Southwest Museum Papers, no. 10 (Los Angeles, 1936),

p. 21: "The crooning to little children is not dignified by the name of singing." Merriam notes also that there are no children's songs among the Flathead. Children participate in adult song and dance, but move into the adult world through their acquired songs and the vision quest (*Ethnomusicology of the Flathead Indians*, p. 26). As an aside, let me say I was interested to find that Densmore goes some way to explaining my puzzlement over the fact that although Grinnell and John Stands in Timber say that the Cheyenne had many songs, I had not been able to locate more than a handful. "Many Cheyenne songs are lost," Densmore noted, with "only a tradition of them remaining." (In recent conversation, Dr. Roxanne Dunbar Ortiz suggested that many songs went into the Native American Church.)

6   *Ethnomusicology of the Flathead Indians*, p. 3.

7   *Teachings from the American Earth* (New York, 1975), p. xvi.

8   Many Indian songs in various cultures were in a foreign language. To note just two examples: a good number of Peyote songs are entirely or partly in a foreign tongue—see David P. McAllester, *Peyote Music* (New York, 1949), and Dorsey and Voth note that a "great percentage" of Hopi songs are "only partly understood" by the Hopi themselves in such important celebrations as the Powamu ceremony. See the *Oraibi Soyol Ceremony*, by George A. Dorsey and H. R. Voth, Field Columbian Museum Publication 55, Anthropological Series, vol. III, no. 1 (Chicago, 1901).

9   *Teachings from the American Earth*, p. xvii.

10   *Roots of Lyric: Primitive Poetry and Modern Poetics* (Princeton, 1978). It should be noted, however, that my remarks on inspiration, as they apply to the Native American situation, may be mistaken, a result of 'Western' thinking. In his fascinating book, *The Image of the New World* (London, 1979), Gordon Brotherston notes that the poets of the Aztec Brotherhood referred to their poems as perfect plants, while their word for poetry, *xochicuicatl* or flower song, stems from the some idea. This idea is most highly developed in the *xopan-cuicatl*, or burgeon song, where not just the poem is the flower, but the poet himself is, "erect and resplendent." That is, "through his art he acquires the essence of the perfect substance maize or embodies the plant which has enhanced his sensation or expanded his consciousness, cocoa or peyote, for example. Like his creation he is shaped from within, genetically and organically. In the 'burgeon' mode of Nahua poetry, as in the American cosmogonical doctrines of man's vegetal essence which it implies, there is far less emphasis on inspiration, on the breath from outside filling the poet like an empty vessel, than on growth from within" (262–63).

11   On the question of translation and related topics see: H. Davis Brumble III, "Indian Sacred Material: Kroeber, Kroeber, Waters, and Momaday"; Jeffrey Huntsman, "Traditional Native American Literature: The Translation Dilemma"; Paul G. Zolbrod, "Poetry and Culture, the Navajo Example"; Karl Kroeber, "The Wolf Comes: Indian Poetry and Linguistic Criticism"; John Bierhorst, "American Indian Verbal Art and the Role of the Literary Critic"; Dennis Tedlock, "On the Translation of Style in Oral Narrative"; Dell Hymes, "Victoria Howard's 'Gitskux and his Older Brother'," all in *Smoothing the Ground: Essays on Native American Oral Literature*, ed. Brian Swann (Berkeley, 1983).

12   Thomas L. McKinney. *Memoirs, Official and Personal* (Lincoln, 1973; originally published in 1845), p. 84.

13   "Chakwena Songs of the Zuni and Laguna," *Journal of American Folklore*, vol. 36 (1924), p. 184. Musicologists since then (e.g., Merriam and McAllester) have collected illuminating remarks from "the singers themselves." For a concise description of how Indian music differs

from European in its systems of pitches and tone, and so on, see Bruno Nettl's essay in *Contemporary Music and Music Cultures*, ed. Charles Hamm, Bruno Nettl, Ronald Byrnside (Englewood Cliffs, 1975), p. 118. And for a discussion of how the Zuni understand their own music and the aesthetics of song composition see Barbara Tedlock's "Songs of the Zuni Kachina Society: Composition, Rehearsal, Performance," in *Southwestern Indian Ritual*. ed. Charlotte J. Frisbee (Albuquerque, 1980). In the same volume, Leanne Hinton discusses how Havasupai songs composed of vocables reveal the songs' deep structure and communicate a people's aesthetic.

14   Alice Fletcher was another who brought her cultural prejudices to bear on Indian music, and agreed with Frances Densmore about the Indian's lack of pitch: "He retains in his song the gliding characteristics of speech. The absence of any mechanism for determining pitch, which would have taught him to treat his tones objectively, may account for this marked peculiarity, as well as for the fact that an Indian song has no established key" (*Journal of American Folklore*. vol. ii, 1898, p. 88). She also believed the Indian had damaged his voice by singing out of doors!

For a discussion of the mistakes early collectors (and some of those who followed) made, see Karl Kroeber's essay, "Poem, Dream, and the Consuming of Culture," in *The Georgia Review* (Summer 1978), reprinted in *Smoothing the Ground*. This essay discusses the real differences between Western and Indian concepts of art; the way in which the Western tradition "has difficulty in making connections between experiences of interior psychic power and external, social efficacies." To an Indian, the dream, the song, entails a transference of *power*. The 'creative act' has to be socially embodied in order to exist. It is energy-conserving and perpetuating.

15   "Notes on Eight Papago Songs," *University of California Publications in American Archeology and Ethnology*, vol. XX (1923), p. 361.

16   "Notes on Eight Papago Songs," p. 364.

17   "Notes on Eight Papago Songs," p. 362.

18   "Toward a Linguistic Approach to the Study of Jazz: The Southwestern Tradition as Case in Point," in Jack Salzman, ed., *Prospects: An Annual of American Cultural Studies* (New York, 1977), pp. 51–61.

19   For more light on this subject, see Ida Halpern, "On the Interpretation of 'Meaningless-Nonsensical Syllables' in the Music of the Pacific Northwest Indians," *Ethnomusicology*, XX, no. 2 (May 1976). She writes: "My field work has led me to conclude that abbreviated words, separated into syllables, are often remnants of ancient words having a certain ceremonial secrecy and privacy which the natives prefer to keep to themselves." One should, therefore, change "meaningless" to "enigmatic."

Karl Kroeber, in "The Wolf Comes: Indian Poetry and Linguistic Criticism" (in *Smoothing the Ground*), also sets out to understand "repetition, characteristic of virtually all Indian poetry . . . a feature little noticed by our criticism because a minor element in our poetry." From an investigation of modern linguistic theory, he suggests that repetition "Is one mode of the process which Jakobson sees as distinguishing poetry." "The 'principle of equivalence' from the axis of selection subsumes the axis of combination," says Kroeber, and in that subsumation he locates "an explanation for the poetry unsupported by effects of metaphor or ambiguity." Dell Hymes ("Some North Pacific Coast Poems"), sets out to show how Indian poems use 'nonsense' syllables for structural function, and quotes Lévi-Strauss: "The function of repetition is to render the structure of the myth apparent." Jerome Rothenberg discusses 'meaningless syllables' in *Stony Brook*, 3/4 (1969), and Jarold Ramsey has noted that "It may be said that whereas in Anglo literature we expect and take pleasure in *redundancy*, in a writer's proliferation of related but differing detail, in Native American literature, both traditional and modern, the emphasis in on repetition. That there is a ceremonial and magical basis for this in Indian experience seems obvious"—see "The Teaching of Modern American Writing as Ethnographer and Critic," *College English*, vol. 41, no. 2 (October 1979), p. 166. Repetition is a form of symmetrical incrementation and balance. Such stress on symmetry, circularity, formal poise, is seen clearest in tribal art—a point eloquently discussed in *As in a Vision: Masterworks of American Indian Art*, Edwin L. Wade, Carol Haralson, Rennard Strickland (Norman, Okla., 1983).

Many musicologists have noted the high proportion of Indian songs without words. There are entire bodies of songs with meaningless syllables. As Nettl points out in *Folk and Traditional Music* (p. 174), the famous Navajo Night Chant, the *yeibetchai*, includes a group of songs sung by masked dancers in falsetto, using only syllables. Only ten of the two hundred and twenty-six songs recorded by Merriam among the Flathead had texts, and most of them were fragmentary. Two hundred and sixteen had "texts of non-translatable nonsense syllables" (*Ethnomusicology of the Flathead Indians*, p. 32). He concludes that the Flathead "do not normally have message-bearing texts" to their songs. His explanation is not structural or philosophic. He suggests that songs with texts were primarily old spirit songs passed down so they became fragmented in time. Since they were private songs, not many are likely to have come down anyway. In passing, it is interesting to note that Bruno Nettl believes words with meaningless syllables fulfilled a role similar to instrumental music (*Contemporary Music and Music Cultures*, p. 116).

20   In addition to the texts, there are records and sound recordings. Indiana University possesses the Archives of Traditional Music. A catalogue by Dorothy Sara Lee, *Native North American Music and Oral Data*, was published by Indiana University Press in 1979. Other important collections are the American Museum of Natural History Collection, and the Frances Densmore Collection at the Library of Congress.

The Library of Congress has issued a number of records made from Frances Densmore's and Willard Rhodes' collections in its series *Folk Music of the United States*. In addition, there are four good record companies which issue recordings of Native American music: Sound Chief Library, Canyon Records, Indian House Records, and Ethnic Folkways Records. Reviews of recordings appear frequently in *Ethnomusicology*.

21   "We Call It Genocide by Energy Development," *New America*, vol. 4, no. 2 (Summer 1980), 37–45. Other essays in this issue address themselves to the subject of profits spelling annihilation. Most issues of *Akwesasne News* devote at least part of their space to genocide by development—see, for example, vol. 12, no. 4 (Autumn 1980): "The Navajo-Hopi Land Disputes: Energy Aspects and Implications," by John Redhouse.

22   After I had completed this book, in the middle of 1983 the Modern Language Association published *Studies in American Indian Literature*, edited by Paula Gunn Allen. This very useful volume contains an essay by Larry Evers, "Cycles of Appreciation," which surveys translations of American Indian songs from Cronyn to Rothenberg and finds them wanting. Evers goes on to stress the fact that "vital oral literatures remain in many American Indian cultures" (p. 29). He and Dennis Carr have made a series of eight videotapes of native singers, storytellers, and authors (available from Clearwater Publishing Company, 1995 Broadway, New York, New York, 10023).

For anyone who might care to hunt for more poems and songs, here is a list of some of the publications which contain riches: University of Pennsylvania Museum, *Anthropology Publications; Journal of American Folklore; Bureau of American Ethnology, Annual Reports and Bulletins; Journal of American Ethnology and Archeology; Publications of the American Ethnological Society;* Columbia University's *Contributions to Anthropology; Bulletin of the American Museum of Natural History; Transactions of the American Philosophical Society; Transactions, Royal Society of Canada;* University of California *Publications in American Archeology and Ethnology.*

Of great use are the following works of reference:

The New Oxford History of Music (London, 1957) and Bruno Nettl's *Reference Materials in Ethnomusicology* (Detroit, 1961), *The New Grove Dictionary of Music and Musicians* (1980).

Likewise the following surveys:

Alan P. Merriam, *The Anthropology of Music* (Evanston, 1964); Helen H. Roberts, *Musical Areas in Aboriginal North America* (New Haven, 1936); Bruno Nettl, *North American Indian Musical Styles* (Philadelphia, 1954); Bruno Nettl, *Folk and Traditional Music of the Western Continents* (Englewood Cliffs, 1973).

There are also two good succinct surveys of Native American music, one by Jamake Highwater and the other by Barbara Tedlock, in *Racial and Ethnic Directions in American Music* (Report of the College Music Society Committee on the Status of Minorities in the Profession, 1982).

A NOTE ON INDIAN / NON-INDIAN MUSICAL RELATIONS

Non-Indian composers have utilized Indian music, though with limited understanding of it. They were drawn to whatever melodic components they could find in a music where melody is a minor consideration, and in which "the *entire sound* of music, its complete tonal and rhythmical reality" is paramount (Jamake Highwater, *The Primal Mind*, New York, 1981, p. 161). Dvorak used tribal material in his Symphony No. 9. Other composers have also used it. In the Frances Densmore Ethnological Library at Macalester College, for example, there are copies of Carl Busch's *Tribal Melodies: From North American Legends for String Orchestra,* published in 1918. There is also the same composer's *A Chippewa Lament.* Both these works were based on Densmore's Chippewa material. Also, in manuscript, there is "In the Vale of Nahwahtonal," for voice with piano accompaniment. Louis Rouillon wrote the lyrics and Maurice Baron the music. This piece was based on Densmore's *Teton Sioux Music.*

The second edition of the *Harvard Dictionary of Music* notes other uses of Indian music by non-Indian composers. Edward MacDowell utilized Indian melodies in his Second Orchestral ("Indian") Suite of 1896. Charles Sanford Skilton (1868–1941) taught at Haskell Institute. Among his works are *Kalopin* (1927), an opera based on an Indian story, *Two Indian Dances, and Suite Primeval* (1920), an orchestral version of *Two Indian Dances* (1915). C.W. Cadman used Indian materials in his *Thunderbird Suite* and other works. We also have Frederick Jacobi's *Indian Dances*, C.T. Griffes' *Two Sketches on Indian Themes,* and Victor Herbert's opera, *Natoma,* all from the same period. In addition H.W. Loomis, Thurlow Lieurance, Howard Hanson, Malloy Miller, Carlos Troyer, Henry G. Gilbert, and others have drawn on Indian music. Perhaps the best known use of Indian music is in Charles Ives'

"The Indian" of 1912, for basset-horn, bassoon, Indian drum, piano and strings (in 1922 it was arranged for voice and piano and became number 14 of *114 Songs*). David Wooldridge has called this piece "a miniature masterpiece, its nostalgia . . . neither personal, nor national, but universal" (*Charles Ives*, London, 1975, p. 166). Ives follows Charles Sprague's poem, written in 1838:

> Alas! for them their day is o'er,
> No more for them the wild deer bounds,
> The plough is on their hunting grounds,
> The pale man's axe sings through their woods,
> The man's sail skims o'er their floods;
> Beyond the mountains of the west,
> Their children go to die . . .

The name of the Wa-Wah Press, founded by Arthur Farwell, was taken from an important Omaha ceremony. Farwell (1872–1952) was a champion of American music which, he insisted, should have an American flavor: "notably, ragtime, Negro songs, Indian songs, Cowboy songs, and of the utmost importance, new and daring expressions of our own composers, sound-speech previously unheard" (*The Wa-Wah Press, 1901–1911*, ed. Vera Brodsky Lawrence, 5 vols., reprinted New York, 1970, p. ix). Farwell's own special interest, as Gilbert Chase points out in his introductory essay, was strongly directed toward American Indian tribal melodies, which he used to break the official, 'German' tradition. Writing music based on Indian music was, for him, as for the others, a vital new experience and a revolutionary act.

Each volume of the Wa-Wah Press contained adaptations of Indian music. Thus, in volume I, Farwell published his own "American Indian Melodies," most of them based on music from Alice Fletcher's *Indian Story and Song from North America* (Boston, 1900). Other pieces are based on Pawnee and Navajo originals. In other volumes Harvey Worthington Loomis published his "Lyrics of the Red Man" (from Fletcher's Omaha collection), and Carlos Troyer published "Traditional Songs of the Zunis," from music he collected himself (he was a friend of Frank Hamilton Cushing).

In *Ethnomusicology and Folk Music: An International Bibliography* (Middletown, Conn., 1960), compiled and annotated by Frank Gillis and Alan P. Merriam, there are a number of entries of musical compositions based on Indian music. Ada Louise Weishaar's thesis contains a section on "American composers who write in the Indian idiom." As for contemporary composers, we might note Charlie Morrow's *66 Songs for a Blackfoot Bundle* (1970–71), and *The Birth of the Wargod* (1972). In both cases, Morrow used English workings by Jerome Rothenberg. And then there are Doris Hays' songs, based on work in the present volume, first performed by The Thompson Street Trio at Symphony Space in New York City in March 1982, and David Amram's *Native American Portraits, Trail of Beauty* (for oboe, mezzo-soprano, and symphony orchestra), and *Honor Song* (for cello and orchestra).

Louis Ballard is a well-known Native American composer. I cannot think of any other Indian composer using Native American material in large choral or symphonic works, but there are many writing protest songs, as well as Country and Western, in English. Indian composers are also writing narrative historical songs in their own language. One singer/composer of note is Floyd Westerman, Sisseton Sioux, whose LP *Custer Died For Your Sins*, is, in the words of Ward Churchill, "one of the finest selections of Country & Western styling to be ignored within the past decade." (See "Floyd Westerman: A Giant of American Indian

Music," by Ward Churchill, in *Shantih*, vol. 4, no. 2, Summer-Fall 1979, p. 59.) The cassette of *Custer* is available from Red Crow Productions, P.O. Box 49, Inchelium, WA 99138.

The New York *Daily News* is not a likely place to discover an enlightened attitude to Native American music, but on July 15, 1983, my eye was caught by a bold headline on page 16: "The Source of American Music." The author was Hugh Wyatt, and these are his opening paragraphs:

"American music has been a melting pot for most of the world's diverse musical forms and cultures for more than 300 years, but few authorities acknowledge the contribution made by the country's original inhabitants: the North American Indians.

"Whether the influences are found in a complex symphonic work or in a simple blues, the presence of the native American is distinct. Indian music essentially is at the basis of American folk music. And with all due respect to the vital contributions from Elizabethan England and West Africa, virtually every form of vocal and instrumental music tracing its origin here has developed out of the diverse musical styles and cultures of the hundreds of tribes and nations of the North American Indian."

Unfortunately, Wyatt doesn't develop this rather revolutionary claim to any extent, but his recognition of "the intense beauty of this music" makes one hope that others will follow his lead. With such notice from a mass-circulation newspaper, perhaps American Indian music is on the verge of wider recognition. (Wyatt spends the latter part of his article revisiting Buffy Sainte-Marie's *Native North American Child*, issued by Vanguard, and Eugene Beyale's *Morning Star*, issued by Eagle Chanter Music, 10 West 15th Street, New York, New York 10011.)

An equally unlikely place to find an enthusiastic review of a Native American musician is *Interview* (May 1984). But *Comin' and Goin'* (Europa Records) by Jim Pepper (Kaw/Creek) received this praise: "if you can only buy one record this month, see if you can find this one." Pepper draws heavily on his Indian heritage.

Just before I finished this Note, Professor David P. McAllester sent me, in manuscript, an article entitled "New Perspectives in Native American Music," to be published in *New Perspectives in Music*. Professor McAllester discusses Indian music which is often issued by Indian-owned companies, music which is frequently Rock-based, or which draws on Gospel and Country and Western tradition. The groups include XIT, and the Navajo Sundowners. Singers include A. Paul Ortega, Eugene Beyale, and Buffy Sainte-Marie, whose repertory from the start has included Indian protest songs. Professor McAllester concludes: "Three hundred years of Indian resistance have finally begun to teach the Anglo world a new perspective."

FOREWORD

There is no safe ground here. Call these songs in Brian Swann's important anthology "versions," "translations," "poems," whatever, no name or act can resolve the tensions and contradictions that pervade every aspect of the representation of Native Americans. Representations created by Native Americans, writing or translating in any of the Euro-American languages (English, French, Spanish, etc.), move differently but are no less free of these problems than *Song of the Sky*. Authenticity is a seductive illusion in this cultural arena. The terrain on which Native Americans and Euro-Americans walk is mapped by inequality. The realities of exploitation and power leave no place untouched. Registered as these are in the European languages through which all the conceptions of "Indians" have been formed and thus moving often virtually unconsciously in one or another part of the culture of the United States, they are especially powerful.

These difficulties begin in Columbus's misnomer for the many diverse peoples of the Americas. His was no simple mistake. His misnaming assumed and articulated a profound set of needs, projections, and ideologies Europeans recurrently brought to the Americas and with which, in fact, they constructed an insistent version of the realities they needed the Americas to be. Euro-Americans have always been fascinated by the Indian, by the fancies their minds created and named. In and through these fancies occasional insight and light occur. But the actual existence, the consciousness, the rich, enormously varied, and complex cultures of the native peoples of the Americas have only rarely been the primary subject of Euro-Americans' endeavors.

So it is that the many first peoples with different languages and cultures become simply "Indians"; savages, noble or bloody; inhabitants of an untouched natural world itself thus reconstructed by European imaginations into "wilderness." The "savages" in the "wilderness" then become either the dream of all that Europeans believe they have lost or, in the nightmare version, the screen on which is projected their worst fears of themselves. To be Indian in this ideology is to be timeless, outside of history, victim, saint, or devil.

Words and language itself are not only at the center of the ideological configuration of this ongoing history of struggle; their very medium locates a special dynamic of power and difference. Spanish, French, English, Dutch, and Swedish were all cultures with elaborated technologies of writing and print by 1492. Most, though not all, cultures native to the Americas lived words and language entirely orally. In their oral practices (I avoid the term "traditions" because, arguably, Native American societies were no more or less "traditional" than European societies which were themselves in great flux) Native Americans created and reproduced an extensive body of stories, rituals, histories, cosmologies, philosophies, a whole repertoire of verbal artifacts, ways of thinking and of knowing their worlds. Many of these have been lost through the accidents of time or the destructions wrought by wars of conquest and the great disease epidemics. Much survives, though in myriad new forms, through complex processes historians, anthropologists, and others are only beginning to conceptualize—by which the descendants of the first peoples have revised and created verbal artifacts in writing and in print as well as in oral forms.

Collecting Native American cultures—material and verbal artifacts, lifeways, belief systems—began with the first European foragers and conquistadors in the fifteenth century. The many kinds of collecting are not only inseparable from European acts of conquest, they also remain integral to the processes by which Europeans and Euro-Americans construct their own identities. Most of the verbal artifacts on which *Song of the Sky* is based were collected in the first quarter of the twentieth century, a few in the late nineteenth or the later twentieth century. The collectors were mostly anthropologists, working a discipline one might say was invented by Indians, though anthropology has yet to get the joke. Some were amateurs, "friends of the Indians," appreciators and patrons never completely free of the inevitable condescension in these roles.

The texts and translations from which Brian Swann shapes his "versions" cannot escape being conditioned, though differently, by the troubled history I have only indicated. Among the anthropologists are many notable for their important contributions to the study of Native American cultures, especially Frances Densmore, John Swanton, James Mooney, Frank G. Speck, and Washington Matthews. And Franz Boas, that protean figure who shaped a generation of scholars and scholarship. Natalie Curtis has pride of place among the amateur scholars in this collection. Only Francis La Flesche, of the collectors and scholars represented, is Native American. Some, like Washington Matthews, could claim great fluency in the Indian language of the originals; others depended on Indian translators. But those with fluency in the language and culture could not dependably elude the baffles of cultural difference. Franz Boas, who "knew the language, folklore, and traditional cultures of the 'Kwakiutl,' or Kwagul, perhaps better than any other white man before or since," nonetheless "suffered from a . . . conceptual tone-deafness, an insensitivity to the categories and interconnections of Kwagul culture."[1]

[1] Judith Berman, "Oolachan-Woman's Robe: Fish, Blankets, Masks, and Meaning in Boas's Kwakw'ala Texts," in *On the Translation of Native American Literatures,* ed. Brian Swann (Washington: Smithsonian Institution Press, 1992), 125–26. This is an indispensable volume, not only for anyone interested in issues

The cultural grids through which these texts and translations are bent on their way to Brian Swann's versions are so many and so intricate that they may always escape even simple enumeration. The reminder needs making, however, that all of these "texts" were originally oral and thus performative, that is, that they were spoken or presented in particular contexts which were as shaping of their meanings as the explicit words. Most of the collectors, anthropologists as well as amateurs, either neglected these contexts or otherwise failed to integrate them with the texts. By writing the texts down, they conferred a kind of finality, the status of a stable artifact, immobile in effect, as though each were a definitive rendering, the authoritative or primary version, while in the oral cultures the telling continued and with it many revisions and creations.

Translation, then, of whatever kind has more than its usual perplexities when it is of Native American materials. One might conclude, therefore, that anything claiming itself as a version could only be a yet more diminished thing. Brian Swann's apt second name for his project in these poems has more than the virtue of forthrightness, no inconsiderable one in this field of mirrors too often deadly in its effects to be passed off as a postmodern funhouse. "I offer," he says, "shadows of shadows." One might well wonder if any Euro-American account of anything Native American could be more. Yet most are much less, more devious and duplicitous by their failure to understand or to acknowledge the politics and history which shape any words presented as by or about Indians.

Authenticity haunts Euro-American thought. The concept has named, since at least the fifteenth century, one of Euro-Americans' primary desires and alienations. The word suggests origins, the beginning, the edenic, the place or state of being before all was injured or ruined—be it by sin or civilization, terms so easily synonymous. One might thus define it as the unqualified possession of something original and thus something unspoiled. Cultural meanings cluster and play profoundly around these terms, ones of exchange and equivalence, of nostalgia and transformation. The "unspoiled," the "original," and "the beginning," aligned on one axis are apparently unambiguously affirmative qualities but they quickly, almost at utterance, suggest an inescapable ambiguity; "naive," "primitive," and "undeveloped" are yoked to them as sibling terms.

These poems do not pretend to authenticity, which is one of their several virtues. Brian Swann in re-forming these various translations of Native American songs and rituals risks damnation for his distance from "the originals" as well as for being yet one more Euro-American expropriating "the Indian." To be sure, he cannot but benefit from the irrepressible appeal in contemporary culture of anything which can

of translation or in Native American literatures, but also for those who wish to understand the Euro-American ideas that have shaped what has been understood about Native Americans.

be named as Indian in its promise of the "unspoiled," of some unalienated social existence, of Nature and a wisdom guaranteed by it. He provides something other than these falsities and panders to none of them. The poems he makes are grounded in knowledge of their provenance, of the full complexity of their mediation by many other hands and a now long history. He undertakes to shape a middle ground between the scholarly and utterly free adaptations. These are sensitive renderings, artful and entrancing. At their very best they may make their readers curious about the rich cultures from which they are derived. Most important, the whole volume makes clear that in reading these poems one does not get to take possession of anything that is Native American. One may have glimmers of recognition—not of commonalties, but of difference.

If the authentic must always slip away, be in fact itself an inherently falsifying end, is everything then acceptable—reversions as well as versions of Native Americans and their expressive forms? If so, Indians would remain figures open to whatever signification anyone chose. Words, their keeping and their passage, have been at the heart of all Native American efforts to keep their own ways against a culture intent on conversion. Keeping lives of their own, Indians had to rely for the most part on their wits and on maintaining their own versions of history and identity in a variety of oral and written modes. The struggle, for Euro-Americans as for Native Americans, is to break free of the imposition of all forms of essential identity. Recognition is the beginning of respect and freedom. Brian Swann's *Song of the Sky*, in knowing so much about the many shadows in this history, is one such recognition. So, too, is the quality of the poetry he makes because it resists any conventional or single notion of "the Indian."

Barry O'Connell

There were hundreds of songs, and they came to
the people in many ways. Sometimes a man made one up, or
heard it in a dream of vision. Sometimes he heard it from
an animal out in the hills. . . .

      Cheyenne Memories,
        JOHN STANDS IN TIMBER & MARGOT LIBERTY

SONG OF THE SKY

Adaptations from the work of Natalie Curtis

Songs Of The Ghost Dance

I
    I saw it   air
        I saw it   the
            the cloth of stars   in
                    floating

II
    dear sister
           Atius Tirawa
           Maker Of All Things
  now knows you

III
    the spirit
           is stirred
                 when night falls
  caw-caw
                I make the call of the crow
      I wait
                  for the stars
      I wait
                    all night
         for the morning star

Nonsense Song To Stop Crying

baby
       floating with the current

little driftwood legs
       rabbit legs
         little rabbit legs

Antelope Song

Wooden spoon
I lost it
My grandmother whipped me

Lying on the ground
Crying
      at the far end of the tipi
                           right by the wall
       and there
           in sleep
      it came to me
         strange power

      now game will always be plentiful

Warpath Song

I am waiting   for my first lover
I can never forget   the playful words you said to me

They all have sore backs   the horses they are giving for me now

26

Geronimo's Shaman Song

through the air
as I move
changing
I go to   a sacred place
this is the way
going up
little cloud   me

Song Of The Mocking-Bird

thinly cloud-covered
sky

mocking-bird

he sings

I walk the straight road
the mesa
to
climb
I

Water Chant

as far as you can see   with me
coming   the Rain-Youth
from behind Niltsan Dsichl   Rain Mountain
now through tall corn
coming
now among swallows
blue and twittering together
coming
through pollen
now hidden in pollen

Hymn Of The Horse

His voice   so grand
               the turquoise horse of Johano-ai

Rich blankets and hides
     hides of the buck, the beaver, buffalo and mountain lion
woven blankets
         are spread
            for his feet
Rich tips of flower-blossoms
            Johano-ai
               feeds him

spring water
        snow water
            hail water
                water from the world's four quarters
Now
    when he walks
         grains of shining dust cloud him
    when he gallops
         the sun's pollen
            coats him in a mist

Now
    the herds of Johano-ai
         increase for ever

Deer Song

they start
      towards me
            to my song
                I am
                   now
               a glossy blackbird
from Black Mountain
              on top
                 where the trail starts
                     coming
             now among flowers of all kinds
            coming
        now in among the dew
      now
    among the pollen
coming
   now
             right there
            the deer
              startled
                turning
           left foot first
            the male
           right first
         the female
   the quarry
   they
      want me

Corn-Dance Song

Who first made
                    shadow?
The Rainbow Youth

            rain   from
    then   behind
Clouds   he cast
        his bright reflection

He-Hea Katzina Song

        young corn-plants
                        in flower
        a bean-patch
                    in blossom
    under blue clouds
                    water will shine
                            after rain

Look
    a throng of yellow flowers
                yellow butterflies
                    chasing
                        one
                            another
                    through the bean-blossoms
                blue butterflies
            chasing
        one
    another

Lullaby

Sleep   sleep

Beetles

on the trail are

Sleeping

on each other's backs

So

Sleep   Sleep

Butterfly-Dance Song

We wrestle for

corn-blossoms

wrestle for

bean-blossoms

we boys

among the corn-plants

chasing each other

playing with

butterfly-girls

we call the thunder

we shall send upward
the young-girl-
corn

thunder and corn
shall grow
together

Hevebe Song

Fat cloud
       come
             pour
                  down

    the   clouds   are   moving

     Gods of the clouds
           break over me

     Make me into a cluster
                   of flowers
     Make me into a cluster
                   of showers

Hevebe Song

             Now from the east the white dawn breaks
Now from the west the yellow dawn breaks
     So now
        get up
     Come look at us
           Your cup of water
             pour it over us
       a cloud
     Come
       pour it over the Youths
        of Dawn's White Light
        of Dawn's Yellow Light
  We make everybody happy

     Here
   are the lives
 of the Young Girl Corn

     Cold water!
     Cold water!

179   Song Of The Game Of Silence

It is hanging
in the edge of the sunlight
It is
a
pig
I see
with its
double hoofs.
It is a very fat pig.

The people who
live in a
hollow
tree
are
fighting.
They are fighting and
there is
lots
of
blood.
The man is rich.
He will
carry a pack towards
the great water.

At the end of the point of land
I eat the bark
off a tree.
I see the tracks
of a lynx.

I don't care.
I can get away from him
along my hidden
jumping-trail.

Yeah!

129

I considered myself
an owl
but the owls are hooting
and now
I fear
the night

142

The old men
say,
"the earth
only
endures."

You spoke
truly.

You spoke
the truth.

That.
That—
whose track
is it like?

Grandfather Two-Teeth
the Beaver?
If it's his
follow it.

The man came to a
wigwam
and
pounded
with worn-out
feet
on the door.

In a wriggling bag
up high
lay a
big
fat
young
buffalo calf
with
a soft belly-button.

There is someone walking
crumbling sticks
and crab-shells.
He danced
a dance
and
knocked his eye out.

The Rain Ceremony Song

The eagle
is flying above
in a round circle
and making a
round shadow
on the
ground

I am
walking around
under that
shadow

The blue hawk is flying in a straight line
and making a straight shadow

Under that shadow
I am running

160

We sit here round our camp-fire
and start to sing our hunting-song

I can clearly see the tips
of the deer's ears on top of the hill

We smoke the flowers of the *pihol*
that make the night clear

so I can see the tips
of the deer's ears

on top of the hill

36

Tule Love Song

Many pretty flowers
                          red   blue   &   yellow
We say to the girls
                     Let us go and
                  walk
             among
         the
      flowers

       The wind comes &
             sways
         the
      flowers

The girls
     sway
         when they
               dance

                         Some are
                     wide-open
               large
         flowers
     and some
         are
          tiny little flowers

The birds love the sunshine & star light
         The flowers smell sweet
The girls are sweeter than the flowers

Yuma Deer Dance

The deer
is travelling down
from the source
of the Colorado River

The water-bug
is drawing the shadows
of the evening
towards him   to watch
on the water

The water-bug   another
is dipping the end   to
of his long body   place
in the water   one
and dancing   from
up and down   and flying
                                 the light
Bobbing up and down   is enjoying
the water-bug   and the nighthawk
comes to a mountain   is up
called Avi'heruta't   Now the sun

Standing on top   the objects around me"
of this mountain   I can make out
he gazes into   "Daybreak is coming
the distance
                                 from his manner of life
He smells the breeze   that is given him
from the western ocean   telling his dreams and the power
                                 of morning
While he is   singing and telling
standing there   And here he is
the ocean
 seems to draw   the nighthawk to sing
 nearer and nearer   The red bird requests

In the water   to watch the dancing
 he sees a fish   and stands some way off
  larger than a sunfish   takes his shadow with him
  floating in and out   The red bird
  with the tide
                                  talks of the dawn
Standing as in   and hoots again and
 a dream   and talks of the morningstar
  he comes to   but he only hoots
   the ocean   whatever he likes
   and stands   requested to say
    on top of   The owl is
    the fish

He thinks
 he is standing
  on dry land

When it moves he says
this place is alive

The water-bug
wanders
along the
sea-shore
forever

38

                stands some way off
                        with him and
                                takes his shadow
                                        The red bird

                                        and the rainbow
                                                into the stars
                                                        He makes dirt
the dancing
The little blackbirds   towards the sky
        are singing the song   and scatters it
                as they dance around   common dirt
                        the sky's four corners   takes up
                                                        The howling coyote
                The red bird is asked
                                to sing   to sing for him
                        but instead tells   the other animals
                        how he lives in   turns and asks
                the clouds and the rain   The deer
                                and says
                        that he dreamed   the ground
                                a dance   falls to
                        that became his   but fails and
                                dance   to dance too
                                                        the raven tries
                        "Such is my life in   in the sky
                        this wonderful air   are dancing and singing
                        but I long to have   While the buzzards
                                children
                        a boy and a girl   the sky
                                to enjoy   singing and dancing in
                        this free air   The buzzards are
                        with me"
                                                                mountain
                When the hummingbird   near the high
                        meets the red bird   lovely plain
                she says she is nothing   gazing on a
                        but a simple   darkness
                little hummingbird   in the
                                                                is alone
                                                        The deer
                She says she tries
                        to enjoy life
                as the red bird does   darkness
                and that she too   he names it
                        wants children   daylight
                to share the free air   After taking away the
                and the freedom
                of which the   daylight
red bird had spoken   taking away the
                                                The deer is

                                                                        39

                                of the ocean
                        forever along the shore
                        Therefore he wanders

                                black
                        and became
                        from the fish
                        caught a disease
                        the water-bug
                        of the fish
                        on top
After standing

Yaqui Deer Dance

of the circle

the middle
to dance in
The deer is coming out

The wind
is moving
among the yellow flowers
of the ai'aiya

on a tree
and hang it
for sure
get the deer
the man said he would

The quail in
the bush is
making his whirring sound

Brother Little Fly
flies round and
looks
at the sun

the deer
they would have
and
this day
out
was coming
They said the sun

The people
are calling
to each
other
and talking

the deer
going to hunt
The man is

Away
in the bush
the deer are playing

the deer
coming after
riding a horse and
The man is

The deer
looks at a flower

song of power
and singing his
sitting under the tree
The bush is

In summer
the rains
come

The grass
shoots up

see the clouds
go out and
40   It is time to

That is the time
the deer grows
new horns

is coming up
The sun

23 : I Dance For The Crops

I dance for the crops.
I dance for the land, for the earth, for many other things,
such as

rabbits
rats
bears
coyotes
and
foxes.
They all get water
from the ditch,
same as the corn and the wheat.

In most places the ditches are filling up.
They fill up full and
sometimes
cause trouble.
Maybe the ditch bursts &
destroys our watermelons
and other things that cannot lift
themselves out of the mud.
But
for the sake of our people
we have to raise ourselves
the best we know how.

Day and night we
try
to wake up.
The only way to be
woken
is by the Mother Cloud
up in the sky.

Different kinds of clouds
get together and work
for us.
They
sprinkle us
with
small rain
so we can move.

So we dance here to benefit
the crops;
fathers, mothers,
all take part in the dance.
We understand the motions he or she
makes in the open air
or in the kiva.
When they move,
we move the same way.

When I grow bigger and stronger, and when
we all stand up, I
shall be big and strong enough
to get bigger and stronger.

90

You only achieve this with old age:
I look like a sea-parrot
with white patches
on each side of my head.

Try to become old as fast as you can.
I look so handsome.

116

This little girl
   will pick black
salmonberries
   when the women
go out gathering
   because she is
a sister of
   Kaka'ochûk,
that little brown bird
   with its
      high
   repeated
      cry

83

I guess you love me
now.
I guess you admire me
now.

You threw me away like something that tasted bad.
You treat me as if I was a rotten fish.

My old grandmother is going to take
her own dried blackberries
and put them
under her blanket.

84

I thought you were
   fine at first.

I thought you were
   like silver but I
find you are lead.

You see me with my head up.

I walk through the sun.

I am like the sunlight myself.

85

I am
        very ashamed of
you for
        speaking through
the fire
        after you are
dead

I won't
        do that
after
        I die

I am going
         to take
an axe
        and
chop down a tree

Song For Bringing A Child Into The World

let
the
child
be
born

circling around You day-sun

you wrinkled skin circling around

circling around you daylight

you flecked with gray circling around

circling around you night-sun

you wrinkled age circling around

circling around you poor body

45

Song For The Dying

Come back
Before you get to the king-tree
Come back
Before you get to the peach-tree
Come back
Before you get to the line of fence
Come back
Before you get to the bushes
Come back
Before you get to the fork in the road
Come back
Before you get to the yard
Come back
Before you get to the door
Come back
Before you get to the fire
Come back
Before you get to the middle of the ladder
Come back

19: Mother's Song To A Baby

First
this little baby
has been given life
through the medicine man's song
through the medicine man's prayer
for this baby the songs
have been sung

Next
the baby's mother
has taken care of him
with the songs of the rain gods

This
little baby
in his cloud-cradle
was watched over
by his mother

It
was
nice
how the clouds
came up like foam
and
as if he
was among them
this little baby
was cared for

On the west side of Laguna, on the
west side, way down, there used
to be a bowl like that in
which the medicine-man
mixes herbs and
water.

It used to give us cattails, plants
and pollen. It used to attract
the rain gods to paint it
with sprinkling rain,
making a picture
of the rain.

Now here above us, from the north,
the duck raingods fly.
They are looking
for the medicine
bowl west of
Laguna.

But a terrible
thing happened.
A
terrible
thing.

Now from the south the winter
wrens come, flying about us.
The birds are white and
as they fly about
look like
clouds.

They are looking for the
medicine bowl west
of Laguna. But a
terrible thing
has happened,
a terrible
thing.

Adaptations from the work of John R. Swanton

5

A man dreams about himself.
He dreams he died.
He keeps feeling he's reached home.

8

I was dreaming of my spirit
under the fireplace.

Under-the-fireplace spirit.

24

I always compare you to
a log with iron nails, drifting.

Just so let my brother float in.
On a good sandy beach let him
float on home.

The sun goes into clouds around you.

I compare it to my mother.

That is what always makes the world dark.

Little Raven, you
son of a slave,
everything you say
comes back to me,
you big sea-cucumber !

You have spots
all over your face,
just like a slave.

I hate to have you
talk to me !

And you're so blind
you dip into sand
instead of your dish.

10

All things,
　　　　all things that live and grow,
all things,
　　　　all kinds of things :
　　　　　　　dog salmon
　　　　　　　　　　he won't kill,
　　　　　　　halibut
　　　　　　　　　　he won't kill.
All things,
　　　　all things that live and grow,
all things,
　　　　all kinds of things :
　　　　　　　cedar bark
　　　　　　　　　　he won't cut,

　　　He won't need to kill
　　　　anything
　　　　that lives and grows.

21

Ha ha!
          Here's where one of the tattoo-marks used to be.
Ha ha!
          Just like a crow,
                         just like a crow!

31

                                             just by sitting.
                                    You are getting higher
                              just sitting there
                         You are getting rich
                    just by sitting
               You are getting higher
          just by sitting
     You are moving
          just sitting there
     You are getting rich
so great as he sits there
     up
growing himself
Here's the chief,

35

          At that time
                    your grandmother's hand
          was hurt by
                    a wooden tray with
          square sides.

                    Perhaps this is why
          you are crying and tossing about,
                    chief-woman,
                              chief-woman.

36

You
     where have you
          fallen
            from

             fallen

              You
            have been
        falling
       falling
    Have you
       fallen
         from the top
            of the salmon-
               berry bushes

           falling

             falling

49

                    from
                  the
                  top
Did you make up your mind to   of
                 a
            salmon-
          berry
         bush
    fall into the cradle

You came to me, you came to
me,
calling
me
mother
instead of someone else.

My chief's child
came to me
calling
me
mother,

Mother of a noble house,
Mother of a noble house.

55

Even dogs
love their newborn.

So I
love mine.

Adaptations from the work of Marius Barbeau

3 : The Lake Will Quench My Thirst

Now the spring will come,
will come and change me.

The lake water is coming, water
is coming which I'll drink.

Where have they gone, those
who went off and brought back liquor?

They are lost now. Now the bottle
that makes sleep is on its way.

Now the train in which
I'll sit is on its way.

My heart is frightened of places
I have only heard of.

Where have they gone, those who
set off and brought back the liquor?

They are gone, those who
brought back the liquor.

Come, old man.
Let's get drunk.

12 : In The Valley

As I sit here in the valley
all the heart has gone out of me.

I threw a stone at the blue grouse
on the side of the mountain.

It hit her, and she flew off.
I re-wove the rotten fish-basket,

fixed it up for use again in the
foothills. But, sick at heart,

I have cut it to pieces. While
I was weaving another, a bat flew

right at me. I will not do what
it orders, the small moth-spirit

that flew at me here in the valley.
Right here in the valley,

all the heart has gone out of me.

14 : Who Will Stop The Sun?

The sun walks about the sky, so
why shouldn't I walk about here below?

Why shouldn't I walk about like the sun?
Why should I only *walk*? I will run!

Who will listen to what I say, as I
wander about crying alone in this

large village? My heart will run
backwards, lamenting. Who will stop me

from getting what I want? Who will
stop the sun when he starts out walking?

Why does my heart feel so small
and speak with such a small voice?

I am small too. But who will
stop me from having my own way?

16: Don't You Walk Too Proudly?

Don't walk so stiff and proud. You
caught just a glimpse of me; I

see you all the time. But do you
think I'll be hurt bad if you

throw me off? You are the one
will come hopping back to my side.

Why do you howl, big Wolf,
while the little Frog plays dead?

Who have you been riding in the forest?

17: Coronation

It makes my heart glad to drink
the fermented juice of small berries.

I mean it! I wonder how my heart
could possibly go without a drink

on May 24. How sad my heart would be
if I should miss it, or let it go by,

when they put the big hat on King George!
In the distance I can see my companion,

getting old and frail like me, she
who I once lost my heart to, my

sweetheart. I will follow her, my
little old partner through life.

I will find the gold teeth she doesn't
even know she has lost yet. And I'll

really taste the juice they all
talk about, the juice of the berries

from Mt. Sadak. (I am very surprized
when you say I got drunk again

on the elderberry wine
I promised to resist).

19: Where Is It?

Where's the whiskey?
It's time to take it
out of its wrappers.
I know you've got it.
I saw it. Fill the glass
only that much—to
the top. That's
enough! Time
to stop pouring.
Wouldn't do
any good
if I
died.

21 : Who ?

"Who made you do what you
didn't want to do, and which
you now regret?"

"That little joke of yours
has to be chased away."

"Look, I have some little green paper
to give you. Why don't we go
sit together at the edge
of Ksimimqh's spring
of fresh water?"

27 : Wait And See

Wait and see what I'll do now.
Wait and see whether I've recovered

or not, sweetheart, before you send
word to me again, you fickle woman.

But do send me something, woman
of the Victoria tribe. A bottle

of Old Tom would do fine. In return
I'll send you these ten beaver pelts.

31 : Wealth

"I paddle on, towing the whole village
behind me"—so an ignorant little man

would speak. But I would never make
such boasts. I leave that for the men

of low rank with rings stuck through
their noses. Everyone knows I am rich.

Something like an arrow sticks through my heart
when I remember the woman I love.

38: Song Of The Sky

I will sing the song of the sky.
It is the song of the tired:

the owl flying down in slow circles,
the salmon faltering in the swift

current. I walk where the water
sweeps into whirlpools. They

talk quickly, as if in a hurry.
The sky is turning over. They call me.

39: The I-Strike-You Song

I strike you. I beat out the uneven pulse
of the song. There is no one to gasp

with surprize when they see me,
when I pretend to jump like a salmon

at the end of the fish-fence meant
to trap men. You cannot see me

as I thrash about, wild and excited.
This is all the Little Humming Bird

is good for. She goes about
gathering husbands in strange villages.

41 : Pretending

Here I am, pretending to be what I'm not.
The beaver pretends to sit down and build

a new dam at the end of the large lake.
He pretends to gnaw all the trees with

his iron teeth, a clever magic-making
spirit. Running Nose sits and pretends

to make a chief of himself in the low
corner of the sky. In the same way

I am pretending.

42 : Who Will ?

Who will chase me into the sky?
Your little song—this little song—

really never rests. You are all
nobodies, you chiefs. You have never

even owned an abalone pearl. The slave
who aspires to be greater than I

is shamed. Stop the chatter, you
of the Luhlim society! Are you

trying to bring the sky's pillars
crashing down about our ears? Who

will run with me into the sky, you
mock chiefs who mimic the real thing?

Will you follow me through the hole
in the sky into the wide bright mirage?

When they see my footprints white
as Raven's in the snow, they will try

to imitate me.

43 : Vision Song (Just What It Said)

Just what did the
voice of the spirit-chief

say about our wealth?
"The voice of the humming-

bird will be heard on
my head in the spring."

My spirit has gone
as far as the Nass's waters flow.

56 : She Will Gather Roses

This little girl was
only born to
gather wild roses.
Only born to
shake the wild rice loose
with her little fingers.
Only to collect the sap
of young hemlocks
in spring. This woman-
child was only born
to pick strawberries,
fill baskets with
blueberries, soapberries,
elderberries. This
little girl was
only born to
gather wild roses.

59: Cradle Song

Sit up at night with me,
mother. Sit up with me
at night to make me grow.
When I'm a man I'll
go where the rivers
flow together, to the
creeks of my forefathers
at Hyanmas, where I'll
catch the large spring
salmon. Then I'll fish
at Echo Cliffs. I'll
gather up the fish-spines
for the old women
to suck on.

I long to be where
the groundhogs live on
both sides of the stream,
where my people set
their snares, where
the hunters cover their
log cabins with evergreen
boughs of the *kanuks*,
at the Place-Of-Snares,
at Half-Leaf where half
the mountain is covered
with trees that drop
their leaves, and the
other with spruce.

But here I wait at
Lying-Across where a
ridge seems to lie in
the path of the creek.
This is the place where
we all live together,
poor, because you can't
go anywhere while you
wait for me to
grow up.

Adaptations from the work of
Helen H. Roberts & Herman K. Haeberlin

Guardian-Spirit Song

it is   making   a   noise

across

the   echo

Adaptations from the work of
Helen H. Roberts & Morris Swadesh

6: Tama Song

The birds are beginning to sound happy
                talking in the spring.
        The Diver-duck is talking.
            When things start pushing through, the
    Wrens raise their peculiar sound, doubling
                their voices, curling grace notes
        back. One knows about it when the tide
    comes in and leaves its mark
                at Village Island, I mean
                    at Yasaayis.

40: Mouse Dance Song

I cause the floors of the chiefs to shake.
I gnaw and carry away all the wealth of the chiefs.
I gnaw and carry away the clover-root of the chiefs.
I gnaw and carry away the dried blubber of the chiefs.
I gnaw and carry away the wild onions of the chiefs.

66: Tsiikaa Song

                    the Day.
                elevating
            soon. I who am
        who am making the Day
Daylight is on my side, I

91 : Lullaby

Sticking-up-out-of-the-water: I am a person
            of that tribe. I am a person
from that place on the water, and so
            my name is
Widebellied-on-the-water.

87 : Marriage Song

Shall I? Shall I have daylight? Shall I
            have daylight on the beach? Where
                on the beach shall I have it?

95 : Lullaby

I guess the
little one
did the best
he could—
the rough-
faced one
whose narrow
face looks
like rocks
sticking out.

97 : Trance Song

There are feathers there on the roof.
            "Make them dance!"
            says the Day.

Adaptations from the work of Helen H. Roberts

1 : Nokwa'nic Song Of Temecula

Over there
        they were looking   gazing from far off,
looking for their son,
            they had come from over there
to look for him at sandy Exva,
           searching near Temeku,
their son,
       searching all over for him.

Then in the east they all saw him, they found him,
in the east, there he was, they all stopped.
                 The Sun—
blackswift found him in the east, hawk found him too,
meadowlark, and coyote, all found him in the east,
they found him there, the Sun rising higher, going on and on,
blackswift, hawk, meadowlark and coyote,
these are the ones who found him there.

2: Pimukval Song Of Temecula

These
they were calling out to us
they were looking at us
they were preparing the
underground house of death
for us.
They found us,
curlews, killdeer, & owls crying
hoo hoo   hoo hoo   oo
turn back. Everybody turn back
west, down to the ocean,
your spirits, your hearts.
Everybody turn back west
toward the ocean,
cottonwood, kelp,
turn back, go back
down, the place of
your spirits, your hearts.

3 : Women's Dance Song

The owl cries out to me,
  the hawk cries out to me
as death approaches.

The killdeer, the mountain bird,
  cry out to me
as death approaches.

The black rattler, the red rattler,
  cry out to me
as death approaches.

The red racer, the gartersnake,
  cry out to me
as death approaches.

A large frog, a little frog,
  cry out to me
as death approaches.

An eagle, a condor,
  cry out to me
as death approaches.

16 : Nokwa'nic Song

Noise sounded
                        the noise   the echo
through my house
                        my little house
my deserted place
                                echo
sounded here in my house
                                        echo
a little   noise
    in my empty place

                                going
eastward
                        it went to the east   climbing
                                                going east
                                                        forever
toward sacred Mixa'lik where it stayed
                                        near the dawn
                                                        forever
                                        eastward   going eastward

18 : Dance Song Of Temecula

They prayed to the night
                nothing   becoming nothing   becoming
                          emptiness   on and on
they prayed to the night
                they named death
they prayed to the night
                bereft
they prayed to the night
                ashes scattered   becoming nothing
                          under the awakal
thcy praycd to the night
                dimness   becoming dimmer   becoming
                          time going on
they prayed to the night
                grey-white   becoming white   going on and on
they prayed to the night
                white   becoming whiter   on and on
they prayed to the night
                covered up   like putting on a hat
stay
        on and on

Adaptations from the work of Edward Sapir

Ruse To Trick The Spirit Of The Snow

"Drive down the elk from their house
    back of the mountain, where they live
black-necked in dark places
    under trees,"—that's what we used to
tell Snow, so he'd stop, and become
    quiet again.

Adaptations from the work of Gertrude P. Kurath

SOCIETY OF SHAMANS

I Marching Songs

Raven
approaches flying slowly
the raven

raven's
voice sounds from far away

raven enters

the ravens
they have arrived

the ravens
are going to sit down here

they sit
in the middle of this house

II Messenger's Songs

The hoot-owl starts u

he is coming to see

he comes flying to see

he has arrived
it is beginning
is it starting from the beginning
the song
it is going from one to the other

duck on the water

drake on the water

raven with the jabbing beak

raven is flying this way

raven with the jabbing beak

raven has arrived
she arrives in a rush
with a rush of feathers
I am trying with my song
she enters in a rush

free the songs
let them begin
this is called *yeidos*

III Throwing Or Individual Songs

In the hemlocks
are plenty of songs

the great *yeidos* ceremony goes on

I took a false step on my way here

I fell down
on my way here

I know all the wild animals
I know them all

they come running for the ceremony
they emerge from the woods

IV Curing Song

Raven
        raven
              he is coming to find out
                        he is coming to see

                                        from the tall timber
                              he is gone into the house
                              he has gone
                              into the center
                              of the house

                they stand at the center of the house

                he goes the whole length of the longhouse

                        he travels
                              from house
                                        to house

V Round Dance

The song,
the great Sharp Point
ceremony
goes on
I see it walking
the song
I see it walking
I went there too
all the others came in
during that song
now they're dancing
the whole length
of the longhouse

We will try too
it is dancing here
my song
we will fill the house with noise
of the pounding of feet
it is well under way
we are turning our bodies
from side to side
we are stirring
we turn our faces
from side to side
we peer about

It has started
we have sung the songs
we have repeated the songs
we have passed through narrow valleys
the bodies of all the dancers are swaying
you are a lucky woman
you shall recover
I know why she took sick
I will cure her
I will make her well
our songs are getting mixed up
our songs are confused
the songs are clashing
our songs

they are walking beneath the hillside
they make a twig stand on end
by itself

like antlers
        their rattles held up
            the masks are butting
                it is peering about
                    the great sharp point

                    the great yeidos ceremony
                        now it has gone home
                        our songs are dead
                        now he has gone
                            above the sharp point
                            let us put the songs high up

                        to side
                            turning his head from side
                            one mask is peering about
                                sparks are scattered
                                ashes flying about
                                red hot coals
                                    the man blows from the mask
                                    their two faces are together
                                each other
                                    our two faces are against
                                each other
                                    their two faces are against
                                    mask and man
                                    everyone is saying
                                    the embers are ready
                                    the maskers say to each other
                                the embers are ready
                                the embers are ready she says
                                they enter dancing
                                the two masks peer in at the door

                        the last song
                        so now
                        now she is dancing
                        I will try to make her dance
                    of the lodge
                    I made her stand up in the center
                    I made her stand up in a certain place
                    I made her stand up
                he is carrying it low down
                they erect a twig
            in the middle of the lodge
        they erect a twig
at a certain place

77

SONGS OF THE WA-XO'-BE

Buffalo Songs

Song 1

My grandfathers are rising, getting to their feet.
They are getting up.
My grandfathers are rising.
I shall go to them, when they have risen,
when the bulls have risen.

I shall go to them, when they have risen,
when the cows have risen to their feet.

I shall go to them, when they have risen,
when the calf has risen to its feet.

I shall go to them, when they have risen,
and come into the light of day.

Song 5

Along the edges of the earth
                              you move
The bull will walk among
                              the visible forms
The bull will come
Among the visible forms the bull
                              will come
Among the visible forms the cow
                              will come
Among the visible forms the little one
                              will come
Among the visible forms
                    in the light of day
                              they will come

Songs Of The Maize:

Song 9

In the newly
                green earth
  in the rising smoke I see
my grandfather's footprints as I wander
                    from place
        to place   I see
      the smoke rising as I wander

            In the middle of all
                visible forms
                I see
          the rising smoke as I move
                    from place
                to place

            In the middle of all
                visible forms
          I see the little hills
        in rows as I move
            from place
      to place

            In the middle of all
                visible forms
          I see the leaves swelling
                as I move
            from place
      to place

The Little Evening Songs:

Song 1

I hear a voice in the dusk
The grey owl is speaking in the dark of the evening

I hear a voice in the dusk
The horned owl is speaking in the dark of the evening

I hear a voice in the dusk
The grey wolf is speaking in the dark of the evening

I hear a sound in the dusk
The snake is moving in the dark of the evening

Song 2

A voice from the dark of the evening tells me to go
The grey owl speaks

A voice from the dark of the evening tells me to go
The horned owl speaks

A voice from the dark of the evening tells me to go
The gray wolf speaks

A sound in the dark of the evening tells me to go
The snake is moving

Song 3

A man is speaking, telling me of my success
The gray owl is speaking
In night's gloom he gives me the word

A man is speaking, telling me of my success
The horned owl is speaking
In night's gloom he gives me the word

A man is speaking, telling me of my success
The gray wolf is speaking
In night's gloom he gives me the word

A man is speaking, telling me of my success
The snake gives me the signal
In night's gloom he gives me the sign

Adaptations from the work of James Mooney

For The Separation Of Lovers

You

Blue Hawk

you hang

high above the distant lake

The blue tobacco has come to reward you

Now you move

and glide down

You have settled

between

those two

Immediately

you have spoiled their souls

They have

at once

become   separated

I am a White man

I stand at the sunrise

The good sperm shall never allow any feelings of loneliness

This White woman belongs to the Paint clan

She is called Wâyĭ'

We shall instantly turn her soul

over

We shall turn it over as we go toward a Sun Land

I am a White man

Here where I stand

her soul has attached itself to mine

May her eyes in their sockets forever

seek out mine

There is no loneliness where my body is

Hunting Prayer

Give me
            the wind
Give me
            the breeze
Ela-kana'tĭ, Earth-Hunter, I come to the edge of your spittle
                            where you rest
        Let your belly cover itself
        Let it be covered with leaves
        Let it cover itself at a single bend
                    May you never be satisfied

        And you
        Ancient Red
    may you hover above my chest
            while I sleep
    Now let good dreams take shape
        May what I do end successfully
    Now let my little tails be made to lie
            in various
                        directions
        Let the leaves be covered with clotted blood
        and may it always be so
    You Two shall bury it in your stomach

Adaptations from the work of George Herzog

Laguna Chakwena Kachina Dance Song

In the place of emergence, inside the house
    of the rain-men, the head of the rain-men
is speaking:
               "Now you are ready to go out,
    you rain-boys and girls. It will rain
all over the world,
    over the south and
over the east. All the rain
    will come to the people.
             Below the clouds,
all the little children are carrying
    lovely flowers. They throw them
down from the sky. These flowers
    are the best clothes we can wish for.
Rain is all over the world."

Piman Flute Song

I am playing the flute here
    I am shaking the woman's heart
I am playing the flute here
    I am shaking the woman's heart

When the sun goes down
    I am making her heart bloom
I am shaking her heart

Medicine Man's Song

here over you   here over you
    there is light
    it moves about
    here over you
    there is light
    the tassels
    downward

Song For Girl's Puberty Ceremony

        over the singing ground
    climbing
The Evening Star is

        It descends
    face down

It moves back and forth
    among the dancers

Rain Song

The water-wind rose way off, far away.
    From far off it came here, from far away
it reached me here,
    bending the corn-tassels.

The water-cloud rose way off, far away.
    From far off it came here, from far away
bending the pumpkin leaves.

Corn Song

When the Earth was
    newly created
songs came for
    the first time,
many-colored seeds,
    low hearts.

Adaptations from the work of Frank G. Speck

Crazy Dance Song

When we ate together,
my wife's mother gave me the edge of her tongue
once too often.
Saddle my mule! When I get
to the wide prairie I'll kill
a young buffalo bull. I'll marry
the daughter of an Osage chief
and make little Osages.

When the morning star rises and grows big,
the old turkey gobbles. When I hear him
I set out with my old gun on my shoulder.
When I get near, I'll climb up
on a large branch. Standing in the tree,
I'll see him. I'll aim at him.
I'll shoot and kill him.
I'll carry him home on my back
to my mother-in-law's.
I'll share the white breast meat
with my sister-in-law;
we'll eat it together. And when
we begin to quarrel and fight
I'll knock her about.
I'll eat all the white breast meat
by myself.

Adaptations from the work of Ruth L. Bunzel

Sayataca's Night Chant

When in the spring
your earth-mother freshens with living waters,
then in all your water-fields, all over,
plant corn, all kinds.
With our earth-mother's living waters
they will once more become
living flesh.
Into the daylight of their sun-father, rising,
they will come out, lifting their heads, stretching
their hands in all directions,
asking for water.
And our fathers will come
with fresh water for them to drink.
Then they will hug their children
in their arms, glad to see them.
They will bring them into your houses
to care for them always
so you can go on living this way
forever.

Now in the rainfilled inner room
of our daylight fathers,
our daylight mothers,
our daylight children,
quietly we set down the seed-bundles
which we brought tied around our waists.
And it is a good thing that,
going only a little way from the house,
our fathers may meet their children,
those called The-ones-who-wait-around:
deer, mountain goats, does,
bucks, jack-rabbits, cottontails, woodrats,
small game, some small bugs, even the tiny ones,
so, when you leave your houses
you may satisfy your hunger
with the flesh of all these.

So that my daylight father's rainfilled
inner rooms may be filled with
all kinds of clothing, and that
the house may have a heart;
so that the shelled corn may be spread
outside his door, with beans,
wheat, and nuts; so that
the house may be filled
with youths and unripe girls
and men and women in the full
flower of life; so that
in this house children may
jostle one another
as they rush in and out the door—
in order that all this may come about
I have placed prayer-sticks fastened together
and put them in the center of the ceiling
          to consecrate this house.

Adaptations from the work of Frank Russell

from CIRCLING SONGS

Song Of The Swallow

Dizzy, I ran into the swamp. There,
      in there tadpoles were singing,
   tadpoles clothed in bark.

     The evening land lay down.
  A deep-blue dragonfly skimmed
      the water. Hovering,
he jabbed in his tail.
        I came there. Saw him
stick his tail into the water,
       flapping, rustling.

I run toward him, I run.
  Darkness rattles. Flowers of the visnago
    cactus in my hair,
      I run, I run
          to the singing place.

from HUNTING SONGS

Datura Song

Morning's first white stood in the sky
    I got up and went out.
    As blue evening falls
I stand up and go away.

I ate thornapple leaves,
    thornapple leaves.
They have made me dizzy.
  Stagger. Run.
Thornapple flowers, thornapple
    flowers I drank.
Drunk. Stagger.
      Run.

The hunter, Great-bows-remaining,
followed. Here he overtook me. Killed me.
Cut off my horns. Threw them away.
Left them.
The hunter, Great-reeds-remaining,
he overtook and killed me. Left these,
my feet, cut off, thrown away.

Flies become crazy. They drop here,
buzzing. Drunk butterflies, butterflies
drunk, they drop here,
      opening
          and
             shutting
                 their
                    wings

from GAME SONG

Football Song

A crowd has gathered. The noise grows.
    I stand, waiting for the ball
to be thrown. I am a swallow
    flapping its wings.

In the far west stands Black Mountain
    round which we run at noon.
Who is this man running with me,
    the shadow of whose hands I see?

from MEDICINE SONGS

Song Of The Black Lizard

The Black Lizard found the trail on which
    Elder Brother had been running.
He came out of the white clouds, following.
    Pools of water fell from his arms.

Darkness settles on the summit of
    Stony Mountain. Circling round
backwards, it scatters over everything.

Reddish snakes dropped like
    spider strings from the west. Stretched taut,
they pulled together opposite sides of the sky.

Quail Song

The grey quails bunched tight together.
    Above, Coyote trotted by.
       He stopped. He looked.

The blue quails ran and huddled together.
    Coyote looked at them,
       sideways.

Mouse Song

Above,
    wings of invisible birds.
 I stand, looking up,
     and listen,
          quietly.

     Floods came from the east
      and washed away our house.
      The earth caved in.
     We watched, afraid. We cried out.
Floods came from the west.
    We screamed,
      terrified.

Bear Song

I am the Black Bear. Around me
   You see the clouds swirling.
I am the Black Bear. Around me
   You see the dew fall.

Song Of The Black Tail Deer

In the shadow of windswept ruins
        I run, trembling.
The wind streams through my antlers
           and over my ears.
    I dash ahead of many bows
              shining, reaching for me.

What horse, what horse will
      meet me from far, trying
          to catch me, catch me?

              Slowly it is lessening the distance
    between us.
        The horse with a star on his forehead
    has come from far to meet me.
How slowly he approaches.

     Here we sit, here, singing
        the song of the east. Here
we sit, together, singing
   the song of the west.

Wind Song

    I came out running, a cup
of water in my hand
    for you to drink. I make you
drink the water, & spin
    dizzily in circles.
Through the white cactus leaves
    I came running. Through
the white cactus leaves I came in
    running, poor, to this place.

Puberty Song

Hurry, come out. Hurry,
    come out. Already
the echoes of night
    are heard all around.
The young girl is sleeping
    but she's not fast asleep.
Wake. Wake. Think
    about the night.

The giant saguaro is
    broken. Broken.
Falling feathers
    gather in heaps,
raising higher the top
    of Mt. Ma-atcpat.

The boy disturbed the stones
    and sent them clattering.
The girl heard, and
    could not sleep.
He broke a nail on
    one of his toes.
The branches of night
    were falling, falling.

As I passed by
    underneath the branches
they tore off
    some of my feathers.

Adaptations from the work of D. Dematracopoulou

SIX DREAM SONGS

I: You And I Shall Go

above
above
you and I shall go
you and I shall go
along the Milky Way
along the trail of flowers
you and I shall go
picking flowers on our way
you and I shall go

II: Minnow And Flowers

flowers droop
flowers rise back up
above
the place where
the minnow sleeps while
her fins move slowly
back & forward
forward
&
back

III: Sleep

Where will you and I sleep?
At the down-turned jagged rim of the sky you
& I will sleep.

IV: Dandelion Puffs

                        above
                   rise
              will   swaying
         of people   like women
    The spirits
                        while men dance,

              swaying with dandelion puffs
         in their hands.

V: There Above

                        spirits are wafted along the roof &
         at the Earthlodge of the South
    there above
There above
                                        fall.
         Flowers bend heavily on their stems.

VI: Strange Flowers

                                    Above
in the west, in the flat of the flowers
        strange flowers bloom,
                flowers with crests
bending to the east.

Song Of The Pregnant Woman

On Baqakilim's north slope
        I was deserted.
Some flower distracted me and
        I was deserted.
A wild orange blossom caught me off guard
        and I was deserted.

Song Of The Quail

I preen myself, I preen myself,
    east of the camp site, where the earth is heaped,
I lie on my back, preening myself,
    in summer, when sunshine falls deep in the northern canyons.

Adaptations from the work of Jeremiah Curtin

SONGS OF THE SPIRITS

Song Of Hau, The Red Fox

I go east on the stone ridge
On the white road I go, crouching down
I, Hau,
whistle on the road of stars

Song Of Waida Werris, The Polar Star

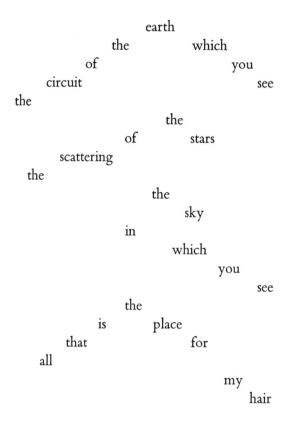

earth
the   which
of   you
circuit   see
the

the
of   stars
scattering
the

the
sky
in
which
you
see

the
is   place
that   for
all

my
hair

The songs of the tribe were coextensive with the life of the people
ALICE FLETCHER

ADAPTATIONS FOR THE REVISED EDITION

Butterfly Song

      butterfly

butterfly

      butterfly

            butterfly—

                Look!

See it fluttering

   among the flowers

It is like a

          baby

        trying to

   walk and

     not

knowing

          how

Clouds

     sprinkle

   down

     rain

Song To A Bee

Flower–fly

      how lovely your sound

            falls

              on the ear

                  You sound

                      too far

                        away

    I am lonely

  lonely

Three Lakota Songs

May the sun rise in splendor

May the earth appear in light

A   wind
wears
me

Look

It is
sacred

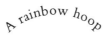

wears
me

Everybody
sees me
coming

Pawnee Ghost Dance Song

Crow
          is calling
Crow
          is calling

Now I am working
in the realm of
Mother Moon

Now I am working
in the realm of
Mother Moon

Adaptation from the work of Franz Boas

Utitia'q's Song

I am happy.
This is good.
There is nothing but ice all around.
That is good.
I am happy.
This is good.
For land we have slush.
That is good.
I am happy.
This is good.
When I do not know enough
It is good.
When I tire of being awake
I begin to wake.
It gives me joy.

The Rabbit By The River

A little rabbit   running by the river—
   Why don't you catch him?
   Why don't you kill him?
   That's what we feel like doing!
               He's
        bent over
           like a little
      old man—
  off he goes
 with a watermelon
        bent over
           like a little
      old man—
  off he goes
with a watermelon

Adaptation from the work of Ruth Bunzel

Antelope, antelope, antelope,
your skin is like cream,
your snout like charcoal,
your eyes like piñon gum,
your sinew like cedar bark.

We Are The Stars Which Sing

We are the stars which sing.
   We sing with our light.
We are the birds of fire.
   We fly in the sky.
Our light is a star.
   We sing on the road of the spirits.
Three hunters among us
   follow the bear.
There never was a time when
   they weren't on the hunt.
We look upon the mountains.
   This is a song of the mountains.

Adaptations from the work of Washington Matthews

NAVAJO GAMBLING SONGS

5 : Magpie Song

Magpie! Magpie! Magpie!
In the middle of his wings are the footsteps of morning.
Day breaks! Day breaks!

14 : Ground-Squirrel Song I

The ground-squirrel in his striped shirt stands up there.
The ground-squirrel in his striped shirt stands up there.
Skinny, he stands up there.
Striped, he stands up there.

15 : Ground-Squirrel Song II

That squirrel, he hit me! He hit me!
The titmice are so angry at this they screw up their eyes.
They grab their quivers.

14 : Dance Song

Although I was eagerly expecting them
    from the east, from there,
although I was eagerly expecting them
    they were not yet in sight—
from the most easterly part,
    the people from there,
and their knives.
    Though I could not see them
I was filled with thoughts of them
when I turned to the east.

Although I was eagerly expecting them
    from the south, from there,
although I was eagerly expecting them
    they were not yet in sight,
the people from Kulusiktok and
    its musk-oxen;
they were not yet in sight,
    its copper too.
Though I could not see them
    I was filled with thoughts of them
when I turned to the south.

    Although I was eagerly expecting them
from the west, from there,
    although I was eagerly expecting them
they were not yet in sight,
    the people from the west and
its mammoth-ivory.

Although I could not see them
I was filled with thoughts of them
   when I turned to the west.

Although I was eagerly expecting them
   from the north, from there,
although I was eagerly expecting them
   they were not yet in sight,
the northern people, and
   their polar bears.
They were not yet in sight,
   the northern people, and
their polar bears,
   the northern people and
their seals.
   Although I could not see them
I was filled with thoughts of them
   when I turned to the north.

16 : Dance Song

Over there, I could think of nothing else.
   Beneath me, where it breathed loudly through the water,
the seal, when it was about to come rushing up to me
   right beneath me—I could think of nothing else.
The harpoon I made, devoted all my attention to,
   When it yanked me violently up and down
over there, I could think of nothing else.
   The caribou—I could think of nothing else.
My friends went to kill the caribou—
   the caribou, I could think of nothing else
over there, I could think of nothing else,
   when the caribou began to walk toward me,
in my pit where I lay listening intently,
   the caribou, when it began to walk toward me.

26 : Dance Song

It robbed me, the wind
   of my coverings it robbed me,
but I saved part of them...
   The wind robbed me
of my coverings.
                  They accept it
from me, they took my song,
   that one song. I didn't
hold it back.
            I held the drum up high,
it robbed me of the power of speech,
   it robbed me, but not until
I spoke first.
            I did not want
to look at that man. I turned
   my eyes away from him.
                   It robbed me,
that bearded seal, of the harpoon line,
   it robbed me. The other sealers too
had not been able to catch anything.
   But I did not let go of my harpoon line.
I waited, and pulled hard.

29 : Dance Song

The animals are beautiful.
There is no song about it
since words are hard to find—
Seals on the ice down there—
When I found a few words
I fastened them to the music—
they left for their breathing holes—
The animals are beautiful.
There is no song about it
since words are hard to find—
Antlered caribou on the land over there—
When I found a few words
I fastened them to the music—
when it crossed the tundra over there—
The animals are beautiful.
There is no song about it
since words are hard to find—
Bearded seals on the ice down here—
When I found a few words
I fastened them to the music
when they left for their breathing holes.

38 : Dance Song

It is pleasant over there—
there are no words for this song—
the animals over there—
Since there are no words to this song—
the animals—
I simply improvise words for it:
a big bull caribou
at Kitinguyaq over there,
a big one, with a big head, big antlers,
antlers large enough to make a snow-shovel,
over there.

52 : Dance Song

He constantly bends it, constantly shoots it straight,
the big bow, he constantly shoots it straight.
He constantly bends it, constantly shoots it straight.
As he searches for a subject for his song
the big bow, he constantly shoots it straight.
He constantly bends it as he walks along.
In summer as he walks along,
it is evidently easy to hit big birds
as he carries his pack, walking along.

53 : Dance Song

Since I was longing for it
   I gave it a name, the spirit.

Blood suddenly pours from my nose.
   Since I recognized this spirit, I gave it a name.

I have not finished my song, however.
   Where has Kaniraq my little sister gone?

Blood suddenly pours from me.
   Where has my little sister gone?
     I have not finished my song.

74 : Dance Song

Me . . .
    It makes
me
      tremble with fear.
                        I have
no idea where my children are.
Since my companions have hidden themselves
I have no idea where my children are.
It makes me tremble with fear as I try to reach Savikyukuk,
as I try to reach it.
I am thinking: a knife.
The needle ice makes it hard for me to travel.
I am trembling with fear as I try to reach Kanuyaryuk,
as I try to reach . . .
A woman's knife.
Me . . .
    It makes
me
      tremble with fear.

123 : Dance Song

I want to laugh, I, I want to laugh
   because my sled is smashed,
because its ribs are shattered,
   I want to laugh.

Here at Talaviriyak I ran into
   hummocky ice: my sled capsized.
I want to laugh. It is not
   something to laugh about.

NOTES TO VERSIONS

from THE INDIANS' BOOK, by Natalie Curtis (New York, 1907, reprinted 1923).

SONGS OF THE GHOST DANCE I

This is the song Eagle Chief (Pawnee: Letekots-Lesa) heard in his sleep, when he saw the night sky and its stars, and the stars spangled like the American flag.

SONGS OF THE GHOST DANCE II

During the performance of the Ghost Dance, Atius Tirawa, the Supreme Being, "a mighty power in human form [who] cannot be seen or heard or felt except through sixteen lesser powers," (Tedlock and Tedlock, *Teachings*, p. xvii), touched a woman in a trance. Afterwards, whenever Ghost Dances were held, people would ask her to join them, and sing this song.

SONGS OF THE GHOST DANCE III

The Ghost Dancers gather at sunset and dance all night until the rising of the Morning Star. The crow is the sacred bird of the Ghost Dance. (Curtis gives a fourth song, but I have omitted it).

For the Ghost Dance, see James Mooney, *The Ghost Dance Religion and the Sioux Outbreak of 1890*. Fourteenth Annual Report of the Bureau of American Ethnology, (1896).

NONSENSE SONG TO STOP CRYING

(Kiowa)

ANTELOPE SONG

This Kiowa song explains how a rite originated—the ceremony was only performed when the need for food was great.

WARPATH SONG

Horses are brought by young men to the father of the girl they want to marry, (Kiowa).

GERONIMO'S SHAMAN SONG

The great leader was between seventy and eighty when he sang this song for Curtis. He was shaman as well as warrior, and this is what he told Curtis: "The song that I will sing is an old song, so old that none knows who made it. It has been handed down through generations and was taught to me when I was but a little lad. It is now my own song. It belongs to me. This is a holy song (medicine song), and great is its power. The song tells how, as I sing, I go through the air to a holy place where Yusun (the Supreme Being) will give me power to do wonderful things. I am surrounded by little clouds, and as I go through the air I change, becoming spirit only." He made a drawing of his song.

The circle, Curtis says, symbolizes Geronimo's changed form, surrounded by a mystical aureole. The sun symbolizes the holy place, decorated with a horned head-dress of divine power. Such a head-dress is the insignia of the shaman. In conversation with me, however, Inés Talamantez questioned this interpretation, and referred me to Morris Edward Opler's *An Apache Life-Way*. Geronimo was a Chiricahua Apache (the people Opler was writing about). On page 311 I read: "The shamans of the war ceremony made hats. These went with the shields. These hats were of buckskin. Some were round and decorated all round the rim. Some were colored black and white and were designed with serrated figures, four-pointed stars, and lightning symbols." The reproduction of two ceremonial hats for protection in war seems to show lightning symbols. Dr. Talamantez says the Apache do not use a horned head-dress, so perhaps the "head-dress" is, in fact, a war-ceremony hat.

SONG OF THE MOCKING BIRD

Of this Yuman song Curtis says: "The meaning is only implied, not fully expressed by the words of the song, but the Indian understands all that lies behind the few syllables." "I walk the straight road" means "I am good and happy."

WATER CHANT

Song from a ritual called the "Water, or Rain, Chant." Niltsan Dsichl is a mountain west of Zuni, the home of the Rain-Youth. The latter made the rain songs and gave them to the Navajo. Pollen is an emblem of peace and fertility.

HYMN OF THE HORSE

Johano-ai is the Navajo Supreme Being, the Sun. He has five horses: turquoise, white shell, pearl shell, red shell, and coal-color. Johano-ai is said to be riding the turquoise, or white shell, or pearl shell horse when there are clear skies. When it storms, he is on his red shell horse, or the coal horse. The *naskan* spread under the horse's feet are woven blankets, richly decorated. The waters the horses drink are holy waters used in Navajo rites. The dust raised by the horses' feet is *pitistchi*, glittering mineral grains (mica?) also used in ceremonies. When the horse of Johano-ai runs, the sacred pollen offered the sun-god envelops him. (Note that the Navajo singer of this song stands among his horses scattering pollen and singing for the health and protection of his animals). This song is used by Ruth Finnegan in her book *Oral Poetry* (Cambridge, England, 1977, p. 103) to illustrate the use of repetition as a structural principle. (I have not followed the antiphonal style of Curtis' translation). For a discussion of other patterns in Indian poems, such as the use of assonance in the Piman tradition, see N. Barnes, "American Indian Verse: Characteristics of Style," *Bulletin of the University of Kansas, Humanistic Studies*, vol. 2, no. 4, (1932).

DEER SONG

One of the most famous of the songs collected by Curtis. It appears in a number of later anthologies, including A. Grove Day's *The Sky Clears*.

Hastyeyalti is God of the Sunrise, as well as God of the Game. He made hunting songs and handed them down to the Navajo. On a hunt, a man first prays to this god, then sings his hunting songs. In this particular song, the hunter likens himself to the blackbird, friend of the deer. The blackbird, say the Navajo, sometimes makes a nest between the deer's horns.

CORN DANCE SONG

The Zuni phrase for "makes a shadow" could also mean "paint a picture." I might defend my version by saying that the Rainbow Youth's shadow is his picture. (A note on Zuni/Zuñi. Taking a cue from Dennis Tedlock's remark that the English-speaking residents of the Zuni area use "Zuni," I too go tilde-less. See "On the Translation of Style in Oral Narrative," *Journal of American Folklore*, vol. 84, 1971, p. 115.)

HE HEA KATZINA SONG

Katzinas are intermediary deities who bring Hopi prayers to the gods. The Hopi impersonate them at ceremonies; masks are worn on which a rainbow is painted. Faces are painted for the ceremonial dance. In the song butterflies in flight over the corn have also painted themselves with pollen.

LULLABY

One of the oldest Hopi songs. One must know that in Hopi-land, beetles carry one another on their backs, and that a Hopi mother binds her baby on a board to sleep while she rocks it. The Hopi say: "The beetles are blind; the beetles are sleeping." There is a longer version of this song recorded by Rhodes on LC recording AAFS L43.

BUTTERFLY DANCE SONG

Young corn plants are called "corn-maidens". This song is part of a Hopi dance celebration by young men and women, beginning at noon and ending at dusk. The girls wear wooden tablets on their heads, symbolizing clouds, and carry sprigs. They are called "butterfly-girls". The young men shake rattles and use a springy step.

HEVEBE SONG

"Hevebe" is an archaic Hopi word, perhaps meaning a certain cloud-deity. This is a song from a game, and an invocation of rain. At dawn, boys and men go through town calling to the people to pour water on them. They call themselves "Youths of dawn's white light." Because their hair makes them look like butterflies, Hopi girls are called "Butterfly, or Shower, Maidens."

HEVEBE SONG

This is an Hevebe song of the little girls. They go naked in front of houses, clapping time to the song, while their elders pour water on them from above.

from CHIPPEWA MUSIC, Frances Densmore, Smithsonian Institution, Bureau of American Ethnology, Bulletin 53 (1913).

179

This song was recorded by John W. Carl, a graduate of the Haskell Institute, whose mother was Chippewa. The game was intended to keep children quiet as long as possible. The children sat in a circle in the wigwam. In the center were the presents. Someone with an active imagination sang this song as the game started. The narrative went on as long as startling situations continued to be invented. There was no apparent connection between the parts of the story; the leaps seem to have been part of the fun. The "I" at the end is the rabbit-hero of a well-known story. My "Yeah!" is merely conjecture. In the original, the exclamation would seem to indicate that the song ended here, perhaps because someone laughed. Maybe "Whoops!" would be better.

from TETON SIOUX MUSIC, Frances Densmore, Smithsonian Institution, Bureau of American Ethnology, Bulletin 61 (1918).

129
A War (or Wolf) song, sung by Gray Hawk.
142
Another War Song, sung by Used-as-a-Shield. It was sung during or after the fight.

In an article in *American Anthropologist*, N.S., vol. 5, 1905, entitled "Notes on Some Cheyenne Songs," George Bird Grinnell says that Wolf Songs among the Cheyenne were said to have been learned from the wolves, and were perhaps composed in imitation of the howling of those animals. They were "songs of travel, or roaming about, and were commonly sung by scouts or young men who went out looking for enemies, since a scout was called a 'wolf'." They were also sung by men when they felt depressed, downhearted, lonely, or discouraged. Many were addressed by leaders to their followers to encourage them. The same might be said of Sioux Wolf Songs. (For more on the "wolves," or scouts, see Stanley Vestal, "The Hollywooden Indian," in *The Pretend Indians*, ed. Gretchen Bataille and Charles Silet, Iowa State University Press, 1980, p. 65). For additional information on Sioux music see *Songs and Dances of the Lakota* by Ben Black Bear, Sr., and R. D. Theisz (Sinte Gleska College, 1976). The Introduction covers the background to songs, voice, song structures and types, drum-beat types, Lakota dance posture and steps. There are also bilingual Lakota-English song texts, with commentary and bibliography.

from MANDAN AND HIDATSA MUSIC, Frances Densmore, Smithsonian Institution, Bureau of American Ethnology, Bulletin 80 (1923).

103
Densmore collected her Mandan and Hidatsa material in 1912 and 1915 at Fort Berthold Reservation, North Dakota. This song, sung by Wolf Head, is for children. The idea is similar to the Chippewa "Song of the Game of Silence": a situation is made as exciting as possible, and a fine imposed on the child who laughs when the song suddenly comes to an end. The end seems particularly surreal!

from PAPAGO MUSIC, Frances Densmore, Smithsonian Institution, Bureau of American Ethnology, Bulletin 90 (1929).

THE RAIN CEREMONY SONG:
The ceremony takes place in early August. This ceremony was recorded at San Xavier, Seles, and Vomari, on the Papago Reservation in Arizona in 1920 and 1921. This song was sung while four men watched the fermentation of the cactus-fruit wine during the ceremony.

from YUMAN AND YAQUI MUSIC, Frances Densmore, Smithsonian Institution, Bureau of American Ethnology, Bulletin 110 (1932).

TULE LOVE SONG

This song is from Panama, and was included in her notes to a Yaqui "Song of Admiration", to show similarities. It appears in Densmore's *Music of the Tule Indians of Panama*, Smithsonian Miscellaneous Collection, vol. 77, no. 11 (1926).

YUMA DEER DANCE

This was collected near Fort Yuma, California, in 1922.

One of the principal cycles of Yuman songs is that concerning the deer. It is the only cycle with dancing, and one night is needed for the ceremony. Each part of the night has its own songs. My version is based on the *selection* Densmore made.

The cycle is based on the belief that the deer has power over the animals mentioned in the song (as well as others not mentioned). Starting at night (top, reading down anti-clockwise), the journey of the deer is enacted. The song(s) relates incidents in his journey over the land known intimately by the Yuma.

The Deer Dance is usually held in the summer, at the time of a full moon. Both men and women dance. If there are enough dancers, they will form two circles round the basket-drums, one circle going clockwise, the other anti-clockwise, one inside the other. The dancers don't sing.

YAQUI DEER DANCE

This was recorded at Guadalupe, near Phoenix. The Yaqui ceremony is a mixture of Roman Catholic and the native religion. This event was recorded on the day preceding Easter, 1922, and the procession, with various instruments, danced from noon to midnight.

Again, this is a *selection* of the songs. Densmore doesn't report if the circle went clockwise or anti-clockwise, so I have chosen the former, the sunrise to sunset motion. Densmore turned a small part of this Yaqui dance into an imagist poem/haiku:

> *The Deer and the Flower*
> The deer
> looks at the flower.

She did the same to the Yuma Deer Dance:

> *The Water Bug and the Shadows*
> The water bug
> is drawing
> the shadows of the evening
> toward him on the water.

George W. Cronyn published these in *The Path of the Rainbow* (1918), which Mary Austin in her introduction termed "the first authoritative volume of aboriginal American verse."

from MUSIC OF SANTO DOMINGO PUEBLO, NEW MEXICO, Frances Densmore, Southwest Museum Papers, no. 12, May 1938.

23

This song belongs to the *sichti* society, which takes part in the ditch opening. The song is part of the ceremony of Opening the Irrigation Ditch. From the line "In most places the ditches are filling up", the plants are speaking. Later in the song there seems to be a blending of plant and human, through the dance. I found it hard to make sense of Densmore's translation of the end of the song, however, which goes as follows:

"When I grow bigger and stronger, and when we have all come back,
I shall be big and strong enough to finish up and get older and older."

It seems to refer to continuity of the generations. Perhaps "and when we have all come back" refers to succession of crops (the crops would then be speaking here). My version is purely conjectural.

from NOOTKA AND QUILEUTE MUSIC, Frances Densmore, Smithsonian Institution, Bureau of American Ethnology, Bulletin 124 (1939).

90

This is a song of the Makah branch of the Nootka. It is sung by the dancer of a solo dance, when he holds up his hand as though it were a mirror.

116

This is a lullaby.

These songs were collected on Neah Bay, Washington, on the Strait of Juan de Fuca, near Cape Flattery, during the summers of 1923 and 1926.

from MUSIC OF THE INDIANS OF BRITISH COLUMBIA, Frances Densmore, Smithsonian Institution, Bureau of American Ethnology, Bulletin 136 (1943).

83

A divorce song from Skeena River. If a woman quarrelled with her husband, and was sent away, she gave a dance about three days later. Her husband gave another three days after hers. Presents were given out. The reference to the grandmother aludes to the belief that if someone gets lost, someone will touch her when she is almost dead and little mice will take her to a house. The woman will put some wool in the fire, and a little old woman will scrape lots of it under her blanket.

84

Another woman's divorce song. The woman danced as she sang.

85

Despite the sombre subject-matter, the melody to this is cheerful! This song has a title: "Song to a Spirit in the Fire," which refers to the belief that a "ping" made by the fire is a dead person speaking. When the spirit comes into the room, he causes a thought of him to enter the minds of the people in the room. Then he speaks through the fire. A spirit who doesn't want to speak through the fire makes known his presence by trees falling in the woods when there is no wind.

from SEMINOLE MUSIC, Frances Densmore, Smithsonian Institution, Bureau of American Ethnology, Bulletin 161 (1956).

SONG FOR BRINGING A CHILD INTO THE WORLD
After this song, the medicine-man or woman takes a reed and blows down the tube into a decoction of sassafras root, which the mother is then given to drink.
SONG FOR THE DYING
The medicine-man/woman sings the song and blows into the medicine made of ginseng. The song and action are repeated four times. The sick person then drinks.

from MUSIC OF THE ACOMA, ISLETA, COCHITI AND ZUNI PUEBLOS, Frances Densmore, Smithsonian Institution, Bureau of American Ethnology, Bulletin 165 (1957).

19
The baby-carrier was called the "cloud-cradle," (Acoma).
35
This is an Acoma Corn-dance song. It refers to the lake near Laguna which has dried up over the years (these songs were recorded between 1928 and 1940).

from TLINGIT MYTHS AND TEXTS, John R. Swanton, Smithsonian Institution, Bureau of American Ethnology, Bulletin 39, (1909).

5
Composed by Qaq! Atcgū'K after a dream on an island.
8
Composed by One-Who-Is-Disliked.
24
Song used when feast is to be given for a dead man.
50
An "Angry Song" composed by Sēxdagwō't against Little Raven, a blind man of Tongan, with whom he was angry.

from HAIDA SONGS, John R. Swanton, vol. III of Publications of the American Ethnological Society, (ed. Franz Boas, Leyden, 1912).

10
The aristocratic baby will lead such an easy life because he will have slaves to work for him.
21
This probably refers to a place on the child's body where she was tattooed in a previous earthly existence. The delight of the discoverer is clear. Perhaps he recognizes who she was.

35

A woman of this family had a large hand and could pick up enough berries to fill a wooden tray. Perhaps the reference is to this woman. The reference to reincarnation seems clear.

36

This poem is used by Dell Hymes in his discussion of some North Pacific Coast poems, "to show that poems may have a structural organization, and 'nonsense' vocables, or burdens, a structural function not hitherto perceived." Of this poem he says; "Especially since the poem is a cradle song, the exact structure of repetition and variation is significant both aesthetically and ethnographically." This is his translation:

> From where have you been falling, been falling?
> From where have you been falling, been falling?
> From where have you been falling, been falling?
>
> The top of the salmonberry bushes, is it from there,
> You have been falling, have been falling,
> You have been falling, have been falling?

(For the reference, see footnote 1, Introduction).

These songs were collected during the Jessup North Pacific Expedition, winter 1900–01.

from THE TSIMSHIAN: THEIR ARTS AND MUSIC, ed. Viola E. Garfield, Paul S. Wingert, and Marius Barbeau, Publications of the American Ethnological Society, XVIII (New York, 1950).

It is often not easy to follow the literal versions of the songs, and there are parts of the fully Englished version which remain obscure. Sometimes, commentary from the singer himself will help. But then another commentator/translator consulted by Barbeau might well offer a completely different interpretation! So I have tried to use what seem to me the reasonable alternatives, and when all else fails, intuition.

Sometimes the ritual, religious, or cultural meanings are irrecoverable. In those cases I have chosen to make a lyric poem out of the ghost pieces. But even where motives and meaning are vague at this cultural and temporal distance, the emotions are universal. For example, the ritualistic boasting and insults in some of the chiefs' potlatch songs should not be foreign to a society of conspicuous consumption and conspicuous display with the (unacknowledged) aim of humiliating others.

The Tsimshian were a people rich in art—sculpture, drama, music, poetry. They were known for the beauty of their songs, both words and music, and three of the more beautiful tunes are reproduced here.

The Tsimshian used poetry in incantation, hymns of victory, elegies, lullabies (privately-owned), and lyric songs. There were large productions of music, dance, and drama that told of the visits of tutulary spirits or current happenings for the glorification of the chiefs and their lineages, as well as for the spiritual benefit of the spectators. There were songs for every occasion, and some were handed down as the private property of certain families. One of the requirements at a potlatch was cleverly-worded songs with comments on weaknesses or defects of selected guests. The humiliation of a rival in song was as much a part of the potlatch as gift-giving. The insulted rival could retaliate at his own potlatch.

The songs were recorded by Marius Barbeau in the years 1915–1929 on the Skeens and Ness Rivers in northern British Columbia.

3

Composed about 1918 by the singer, Watserh.

12

Sung by Watserh, who interpreted the blue grouse as the wife a man sent away. The song begins after the bat which the grouse-wife has sent has appeared. It was believed that when a bat hit someone he was about to die.

14

(Original title, "The Sun Walking"). A lyric love song sung by Gyaedemraldan of Kincolith, Nass River. It was composed by his father Kawawdzu when he married his first wife, a Gitksan from the upper Skeena. The Nass River women were naturally opposed and jealous, but Kawawdzu was a chief used to getting his own way. (The references to smallness are not meant literally: they are examples of litotes).

16

This song, sung by Pahl, is the song of a woman separated from her husband or lover. In the last phrase she wonders if he's been unfaithful. The reference to Wolf and Frog implies that he belongs to the Wolf clan and she to the Frog.

16—WUTSATSIKSYE (Don't you walk too proudly?)

Key to Musical Signs used in Transcription

Besides the conventional signs which retain their usual meaning, the following special signs have been used:

+ the note following is slightly higher, or intermediate between two of our half tones.

◡ ascending glide.

〜 a long, slow glide sometimes rendered decrescendo, tending to vanish at its end.

〜 ascending, as above.

᾽ over a note means fortis or glottalized pronunciation.

17

(Original title, "How Small".) A dance song, sung by Tralahaet, and composed by him twenty years earlier on the crowning of King George V.

21

I do not understand the second stanza, and the notes do not help. But it is appealing in its reference to something the lovers know, and we do not. Which is how it should be. The green paper is either money or a ticket.

27

This is a challenge song for the distribution of food and gifts at a feast, sung by Tralahaet, and belonging to all the Eagle clan. Sanan'wan, an Eagle chief, composed it after his wife left him to marry an important man of the Hudson's Bay Company in Victoria. He intended to ridicule the woman with the ten "beaver pelts" (they were in fact a fine gift of ten marten skins). He supposed she would be unable to reciprocate, but at a later feast she gave Sanan'wan a big canoe; turned the Old Tom bottle, as it were, into an ever finer gift, and carried the day.

31

The chief sings this at a feast before the distribution of presents. He praises himself and his power, while at the same time disavowing his display. He taunts those of his guests who wear nose-rings as "common." The song was composed by Arhatat, a relative of Tralahaet, the singer.

38

The original title is "I Will Sing". An ancient chief's song used at a potlatch before the distribution of gifts, and recorded by Tralahaet.

39

A Nass River song used by Chief Weegyaet "long ago," when he appeared in his regalia at a feast. The "uneven pulse" refers to the fact that there are three beats, one and two are beaten, while the third is silent.

41

"Sigway," a chief's song sung by Wirhae at a potlatch. As in other songs of this kind, the guests to whom gifts are given are taunted. The chief spoken of in the song is as clever as the beaver. He is trying to "break in" and be one of the chiefs.

41—SIGWAY (Pretending)

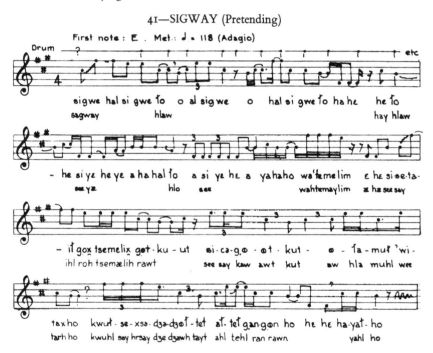

42

When the chief sings this song he dances in all his regalia. He shakes his bird rattles, nods his head, and the down from his crown fills the air in token of peace and friendship. There is the usual taunting, nevertheless. The little song that never rests is a hint to some of the chiefs that they never give a feast, and so their songs are not heard.

43

This song expresses what Hrkwawyem saw in a vision. The humming-bird was his spirit helper. When he was a small chief and still poor, his visions could not travel a great distance. But as soon as he became rich and a great chief, his visionary powers extended as far as the Nass flows.

56

This is a lullaby for girls, belonging to the family of Weerhae of Gitwinlkul, the head family of the Wolf Clan.

56—TEMRAM SAKALAMPS (She will gather roses)

59

The original title is "Dear Boy." This song is the exclusive property of the family of Tralahhaet, chief of an Eagle clan at Hyanmas. Unlike most of the other songs here, it was used privately, and not at a feast, to put a child to sleep.

from SOME SONGS OF THE PUGET SOUND SALISH, Helen H. Roberts and Herman K. Haeberlin, *Journal of American Folk-Lore*, vol. 31, (1918).

I have altered nothing from the original translation, except the arrangement of the words. The *yeyē'i* is supposed to imitate the sound of the echo. The collectors note: "This charming little song has all the mystery that echo inspires, and the echo itself is part of the melody. One can well imagine it occupying a fitting position among collections of folk-songs for children."

GUARDIAN SPIRIT SONG

At this point, it might be worth noting the wide range of musical styles among the North American Indians. Roberts and Haeberlin note that the Salish, for instance, use a far more "Occidental" scale system than, say, the Sioux. And Gertrude Kurath in *Iroquois Music and Dance*—see later—had difficulty transcribing melodies. She abandoned signatures "as unsuited to the Indians' musical perception," and noted that "any metrical divisions are arbitrary and perforce tentative." Many earlier collectors simply flattened out the Indian melody, making it acceptable to "Western" ears.

from SONGS OF THE NOOTKA INDIANS OF WESTERN VANCOUVER ISLAND, Helen H. Roberts and Morris Swadesh, Transactions of the American Philosophical Society, n.s. vol. 45, part 3 (1955).

These songs were originally collected by Edward Sapir in 1910 and 1913-14.

6 : TAMA SONG

"Tama" implies a festivity, and such songs are often sung at potlatches. They are among the least formal types of songs; some are ceremonial and some are purely family songs. This song was composed by Kwiiku-wuth as he was sitting on the beach in early spring and feeling happy. The grammatical form used for Diver-duck and Wren is used when speaking of or to myth characters, or people having special characteristics. I have used capital letters to indicate something special about the birds.

40 : MOUSE DANCE SONG

This song accompanies the Mouse imitative dance in the Wolf ritual. When I first read it I thought the song was a meditation on mortality, and the vanity of earthly goods. But then I discovered that the activity of the mouse is symbolic of the distribution of wealth by powerful chiefs.

66 : TSIIKAA SONG

Tsiikaa songs are used for marriage ceremonies. This song refers to the supernatural

Breakers-people who are supposed to pray thus to the Day. Marriage tsiikaa are prayerful rather than boastful.

91 : LULLABY

This song was used only for boys, and refers to the young sea-otters who float on the sea belly up.

87 : MARRIAGE SONG

This song was obtained in a dream. In the dream there were dancers representing the sun.

95 : LULLABY

The purpose of this song is to make the baby's narrow face broad and flat, the Nookta ideal of beauty.

97: TRANCE SONG

Sung by the diviner, eyes shut.

from Helen H. Roberts' *FORM IN PRIMITIVE MUSIC* (New York, 1933).

1 : NOKWA'NIC SONG OF TEMECULA

The songs in this section are from the Luiseño and Gabrielino Indians of Southern California (the names are derived from the missions to which they were attached). They were (and are) Shoshonean people. The songs excerpted here occur in religious ceremonies. This song is related to the Creation Myth, and such songs are called *mo'nivul*, "songs of travel," since they relate the wanderings of the people after they emerged from the underground darkness where they were born and began finding places for themselves on earth. The term "nokwa'nik," used by the singer, Flora Pa'henim of Pala, is obscure.

Temecula (Temeku) is in Luiseño territory, inland between San Diego and Los Angeles. The area is the center of many myths, and the name Temecula seems related to "teme," the Sun, and might mean "where the Sun first rose."

Flora Pa'henim explained the song: "At first they were in the dark. And they were looking for their son, and their son was the Sun and they found him as he arose." The Sun, that is, departed to give light to his people.

For more on Southern California Indians, see A. L. Kroeber, *Handbook of the Indians of California* (Bulletin 78, Bureau of American Ethnology, Washington, 1923). For an excellent, scathing account of the missions, read Carey McWilliams' *Southern California Country* (New York, 1946), and for a romantic apologia see *Capistrano Nights*, by Charles Francis Saunders and Father John O'Sullivan (New York, 1930).

2 : PIMUKVAL SONG OF TEMECULA

It is hard to put together versions of these songs since the collector herself acknowledged her own shortcomings with the language, and the short time she had to record. Any version must be tentative. Still, one can get a glimpse at the meaning, though I have cut down on repetition and interweaving of phrases.

Flora Pa'henim explained the song thus: "This is an old song which tells about the birds. They first found out about the beginning of death to man. The people in this country believe that whenever birds come in the house death is coming. These birds would come, and that is why they say they found death for man."

The song seems to be a *pimukval* or death song, sung during the burning of the dead person's clothes. Or it may have been used in the Eagle-killing ceremony, a ceremony seemingly connected to the myth of Woyo'te, a semi-divine being, "el padre de nosotros," as Celestino Awai'u of Pichanga explained.

In this song the birds which found death are calling out the command for all spirits to turn west when they depart. Flora Pa'henim said people thought that if they went to the ocean they might be spared death. They called upon cottonwood and kelp to help them in a spirit way, so perhaps they wouldn't die. It seems also as if the birds are telling the people to turn back, and to call on cottonwood and kelp to deliver them from death.

3 : WOMAN'S DANCE SONG

This song belonged to the grandfather of Celestino Awai'u, who sang it for Roberts. Helen Roberts writes: "In this song it was explained that the animals were bidding goodbye to the person" about to die. "Gartersnake" is surmise on my part from the description provided (like a red racer but larger, and with two white stripes). The gartersnake's stripes, however, are more yellow than white. The identity of the mountain bird eludes me. "Like a blackbird with white neck ring," reads the text.

16 : NOKWA'NIC SONG

Celestino Awai'u said this song was "used in a woman's dance belonging to the ceremony called tu'vic." It probably relates to Woyo'te's death, when the birds and other creatures were called upon to diagnose his illness.

Celestino Awai'u remarked that there used to be a man who lived at Huyulkum and who was the leader in the singing. When someone died, this song was sung in his house. The leader could hear the echo in his house. "After he died it all went away."

Songs like this were similar to prayers for the spirit leaving through a gate in the east before dawn. Awai'u, the singer, noted that Mixa'lik "was the name of the place where he stayed." ("He" is presumably the spirit). In the song, it seems that the echo of the singing is somehow equivalent to the departing spirit.

18 : DANCE SONG OF TEMECULA

This song relates to the burning of the dead, perhaps to the cremation of Woyo'te. The "avakal" was the slightly hollowed piece of wood placed over the corpse. The covering, toward the end, "like putting on a hat," seems to refer to the body or the ashes covered with the avakal.

The song looks to be in two parts: the refrain describing the action of the mourners, and the lines describing the corpse.

Helen H. Roberts was one of the earliest collectors/scholars to attempt to hear Indian songs as they are. She stressed their wide variety of musical styles and ability of the singers. She was wary about large generalizations concerning quality, generalizations which had been made without adequate knowledge of languages, conventions, cultures. She called for an open, adventurous spirit: "Failure to perceive fascinating complexities may lie . . . in an obtuse and still too orthodox viewpoint." After all, she noted, Indians had anticipated our twentieth century musical revolution in throwing off the shackles of orthodox major and minor keys. See *Musical Areas in Aboriginal North America*, Yale University Publications in Anthropology, no. 12, (1936), 3-41.

from RELIGIOUS IDEAS OF THE TAKELMA INDIANS OF SOUTHWEST-ERN OREGON, Edward Sapir, *Journal of American Folklore*, vol. 20, (1907).

Originally, this was a charm or prayer. The Spirit of the Snow, though he drove down deer from the mountains, was not believed to be particularly well-disposed, and begrudged man game. When it snowed too heavily, the Spirit of the Snow was brought to a halt by a ruse that relied on his niggardly nature.

from IROQUOIS MUSIC AND DANCE: CEREMONIAL ARTS OF TWO SENECA LONGHOUSES, Gertrude P. Kurath, Smithsonian Institution, Bureau of American Ethnology, Bulletin 187 (1964).

The *yeidos* (more accurately, *ʔi:do:s*) ceremony is also called the Society of Medicine Men and Mystic Animals. It is a curative ceremony, which takes place at night in the patient's home, or, less frequently, during medicine rite renewals of Midwinter Festivals, and at special meetings three times a year: June, September, Midwinter.

The animals evoked in the early songs are the sacred animals who had originally taught the shamans the songs. Their presence was necessary for the rites to be performed properly, and the continued good will of the "medicine animals" was absolutely necessary.

I would like to thank Prof. William N. Fenton for putting me right in a number of places, and some helpful remarks which I have incorporated into these notes. Needless to say, any mistakes are my own.

I am also indebted to his "Tonawanda Longhouse Ceremonies: Ninety Years After Lewis Henry Morgan," Bureau of American Ethnology, Bulletin 128 (1958), and "Masked Medicine Societies of the Iroquois," *Annual Report of the Smithsonian Institution*, 1940. See also Arthur C. Parker, "Secret Medicine Societies of the Seneca," *American Anthropologist*, n.s., vol. 11, no. 2, (April-June, 1909).

Kurath did her site work at the Coldspring longhouse in the late 1940's.

I MARCHING SONGS

There are five songs in the ceremony, sung by the entire company of between 12 and 15 men, all shaking gourd rattles, and dancing, "marching" from an adjoining house to the ritual site. I refer the reader to Kurath for a complex description of dance, music, ceremony, action.

II MESSENGER'S SONGS

Fifteen songs in groups of twos and threes. The song "going from one to the other" means that the men sitting there sing in rotation, counterclockwise.

III THROWING OR INDIVIDUAL SONGS

Solos: individual songs, individual singers, any number—eight were recorded. Again, the singing moves anticlockwise. The singers rise from time to time and dance. Opposite moieties sit across the fire. Each song is sung twice, with rattle tremulo.

IV CURING SONGS

Ten songs sung by Messenger and helper. Each song is sung twice.

V ROUND DANCE

I have tried to incorporate in the text some of the ritual action. The participants in the

Round Dance are the sponsor, two masked figures, and the assembly. Some of the songs refer to feats of magic which are no longer performed—tossing hot rocks, casting the sharp point (whatever it was), making the twig stand erect in the middle of the lodge, and perhaps Kurath's enigmatic "rattles stood on end of handle several feet above floor". At some point, they put the songs on high, overhead—in the old longhouses there was a shelf over the bunks where gear was stored.

In the Round Dance there is use of masks, those of the so-called False Faces, the society that cured disease and sickness, especially diseases of the face and head. They would perform shamanistic acts, such as juggling live coals, and blew hot ashes over the affected part or the sick person. Their rattles were made of the shells of snapping turtles.

For more on Iroquois ceremonial, see Frank G. Speck, *Midwinter Rites of the Cayuga Longhouse* (Philadelphia, 1949), and Elizabeth Tooker, *The Iroquois Ceremonial of Midwinter* (Syracuse, 1970).

from THE OSAGE TRIBE: RITE OF THE WA-XO'-BE, Francis La Flesche, Bureau of American Ethnology, 45th. Annual Report, 1927-28.

The Wa-Xo'-Be is a rite of cosmic character, "a dramatization," says La Flesche, "of the movements of certain cosmic forces whose combined power brought forth material life upon the earth and set it in perpetual motion."

BUFFALO SONGS

SONG 1

This song refers to the coming of the buffalo from the mysterious invisible world into the material and visible world. First come the full procreative powers of male and female, then the birth of the calf, and finally completion and full appearance. The first song, notes La Flesche, "indicates a thoughtful, contemplative mood, having for its object the performance of an act that will greatly affect the welfare of the people; the music of the song expresses dignity, solemnity, and a reverence for the power that gives thought to a vast and far-reaching movement."

SONG 1

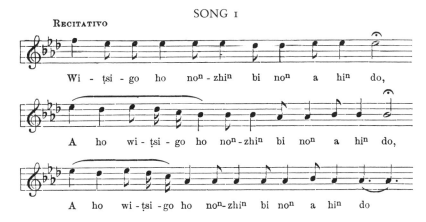

RECITATIVO

Wi - tsi - go ho noⁿ - zhiⁿ bi noⁿ a hiⁿ do,

A ho wi - tsi - go ho noⁿ - zhiⁿ bi noⁿ a hiⁿ do,

A ho wi - tsi - go ho noⁿ - zhiⁿ bi noⁿ a hiⁿ do

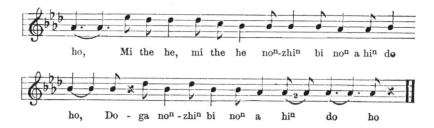

ho,   Mi the he, mi the he non-zhin bi non a hin do

ho,   Do - ga non-zhin bi non a   hin   do   ho

SONG 5

"In many of the Siouan tribes there are rites by which the people call the buffalo to come to their aid in the struggle to maintain life. From the words of the ritual songs of this character a stranger who is not familiar with the Indian ceremonial mode of thought and expression would fall into the belief that the supplications for aid were addressed to the animal itself, but a closer, thoughtful study would lead him to the understanding that the call for aid was made through the animal to the Mysterious Power that gave it life and form.

The ancient Non'-hon-zhin-ga who composed these songs mention the buffalo in the sequential order of their creation as dictated to them by wa-thi'-gthon, or a carefully studied reasoning, namely, the male first, the female next, and lastly the little one. While by the final stanza they call the three in their triple relationship to come into the light of day, the call is, in reality, a song of adoration of the power that made the light of day for the benefit of all living creatures," (La Flesche).

Song 5 is the approach of the buffalo to the world of sight and touch. The words and music denote happiness and faith that the buffalo have come for all time.

SONG 5

Mon - in - kau - hon - ge dsi tha thin - she non, Tho -

ge non do - ga gi ta bi the the he the, Do - ga gi ta bi the

the, Tho - ge non do - ga gi ta bi the the he.

SONGS OF THE MAIZE

SONG 9

In the ceremony, the Songs of the Maize follow the Buffalo Songs. The buffalo and the maize are two sacred forms of life, animal and vegetable.

"The words and the music of the song express joy at the awakening of the earth from its long winter sleep; the smoke arising from the fields where the women are preparing the soil for planting; the sight of the long rows of little hills within which are to be put the precious seeds from which the people hope for a rich harvest; the sight of the young stalks as they spread their blades in the winds and take their place amid other living forms; the sight of the bright light of day that touches every form of life and urges each onward toward maturity," (La Flesche).

Amid all this awakening of life is perceived a first token of the presence of the Divine, Creative Power, a presence, says La Flesche, "that is indicated by some visible mark, like footprints upon the earth's surface."

SONG 9

Mon - in - ḳa ṭse - ga ge non dse . he, Wi - ṭsi - go a - çi -
gthe sho-dse ge, Ṭon - be mon-bthin-e the he the, Sho-dse ge ṭon -
be mon-bthin-e the, Tho ge non sho-dse ge Ṭon - be mon-bthin-e the he.

THE LITTLE EVENING SONGS

SONGS 1–3

La Flesche writes:

"In each of the three songs of the Little Evening Songs the chief commander of a war party is represented as speaking. This officer, who acts as mediator between his warriors and the Mysterious Power that governs all things, travels apart from his men throughout the day and at night he stands alone, far away from the camp, to listen, in the gloom of evening, for the word of approval that might come through the medium of the gray owl, the horned owl, the gray wolf, or the peculiar sounds made by a snake.

It is implied by the words of the first song of this group that the chief commander listens for the voices of the owls or the wolf or for the sounds made by the snake during his nightly vigil and accepts as a favorable answer to his supplications the first one of these he hears."

SONG 1

Pa - çe u - tha - ga . . . . tha tsi - the he
he the, Wa - po - ga-e tha pa - çe u tha-ga . . . . tha tsi -

143

he . . . . he the, Tsi - the he the Wa - po - ga - e

tha pa - çe u - tha - ga . . . . . tsi - the he.

SONG 2

M.M. ♩ = 80

Pa - çe u - tha - ga . . the tse the the he the, Wa - po -

ga - e tha pa - çe u - tha - ga . . the tse the . . the tse

the the he the, Wa - po - ga - e tha pa - çe u tha -

ga . . the tse the, . . The tse the the the he.

SONG 3

M.M. ♩ = 92

Ni - ḳa wiⁿ hoⁿ - da - doⁿ i - e hi - the toⁿ - noⁿ, Ni - ḳa

wiⁿ hoⁿ - da - doⁿ i - e hi - the toⁿ, I - e hi - the toⁿ noⁿ,

wa - po - ha - ga, Pa - çe u - tha - ga i - e hi - the toⁿ

noⁿ, Ni - ḳa wiⁿ hoⁿ - da - doⁿ i - e hi - the toⁿ noⁿ.

144

Francis La Flesche is an important figure in Indian studies. Ponca by birth, he spent most of his life among the Pawnee, Otos and Omaha. He spoke several Indian languages, as well as English and French. He collaborated with scholars such as Alice Fletcher, and became a scholar in his own right. For more on the La Flesche family, see Norma Kidd Green, *Iron Eye's Family: The Children of Joseph La Flesche* (Lincoln, Johnson Publishing Co., 1969). In passing, one might note that La Flesche's work provided Claude Lévi-Strauss with some of his most important evidence in *The Savage Mind*.

from THE SACRED FORMULAS OF THE CHEROKEE, James Mooney, U.S. Bureau of American Ethnology, 7th Annual Report, 1885-86.

FOR THE SEPARATION OF LOVERS

This prayer is to separate two lovers or a husband and wife, and bring about what the jealous rival desires. There is no explanation of the accompanying ceremonial, but tobacco seems to be used. In Cherokee color symbolism, blue brings trouble. White, on the other hand, indicates the man is "happy and attractive in manner," (Mooney). To "spoil souls" is to change feelings, and "turning over a soul" would suggest that the woman's feelings are to be redirected. The phrase is more commonly used, however, to indicate killing.

HUNTING PRAYER

This prayer is addressed to the two great gods of the hunter, Fire and Water. The evening before the hunt, the hunter "goes to water"—for this ceremony, see Mooney, *The Swimmer Manuscript*, Smithsonian Institution, Bureau of American Ethnology, Bulletin 99 (1932). In the morning, fasting, the hunter sets off. At sunset, he again conducts the "going to water" ceremony and recites this formula. He then makes his fire and eats his supper. He lies down, first rubbing his breast with ashes from his fire. In the morning he starts to look for game.

The hunter asks for wind and breeze so the game won't scent him when he stalks them.

The "Earth-Hunter" here signifies the river. The name, says Mooney, "refers to the way the tiny streams and rivulets search out and bring down to the great river the leaves and debris of mountain forests." The spittle is foam, and "let your belly" etc., means: let the leaves, stained with the quarry's blood, be so numerous as to cover the water.

"At a single bend" etc., expresses the hunter's desire that he won't have to search the whole forest.

The hunter is supposed to feed the river with blood washed from the game. Likewise, he feeds the fire with a piece of deer tongue.

"You Two shall bury it in your stomach," refers to the bloody leaves and the piece of tongue cast, respectively, into River and Fire.

Mooney makes no explanatory comment on those little tails, so I can only guess at a meaning. Perhaps the hunter is asking for plenty of deer, in all directions. (Could "tails" be a misprint for "trails"?)

Incidentally, the earliest extensive translation of an Indian song which I have come across is from the Cherokee. It occurs in *The Memoirs of Lieut. Henry Timberlake*, published in 1765 in London (reprinted by The Wataugh Press of Johnson City, Tennessee, in 1927), a book which Robert Southey made extensive use of in the preparation of his epic poem *Madoc*, (1805).

Timberlake came to know the Cherokees quite well, and he includes the following translation of a War Song in his book. He chose the War Song as an example of the Cherokee "sort of loose poetry" rather than a love song because many of the latter "contain no more than the young man loves the young woman, and will be uneasy, according to their own expression, if he does not obtain her." The War Song, he notes, will be given without "the expletive syllables, merely introduced for their music, and not the sense, just like the toldederols of many old English songs."

A TRANSLATION OF THE WAR-SONG

Caw waw noo dee, &C.

Where'er the earth's enlighten'd by the sun,
Moon shines by night, grass grows, or waters run,
Be't known that we are going, like men, afar,
In hostile fields to wage destructive war;
Like men we go, to meet our country's foes,
Who, woman-like, shall fly our dreaded blows;
Yes, as a woman, who beholds a snake,
In gaudy horror, glisten thro' the brake,
Starts trembling back, and stares with wild surprize,
Or pale thro' fear, unconscious, panting, flies.
Just so these foes, more tim'rous than the hind,
Shall leave their arms and only cloaths behind;
Pinch'd by east blast, by ev'ry thicket torn,
Run back to their own nation, now its scorn:
Or in the winter, when the barren wood
Denies their gnawing entrails nature's food,
Let them sit down, from friends and country far,
And wish, with tears, they ne'er had come to war.

We'll leave our clubs, dew'd with their country show'rs,
And, if they dare to bring them back to our's,
Their painted scalps shall be a step to fame,
And grace our own and glorious country's name.
Or if we warriors spare the yielding foe,
Torments at home the wretch must undergo.

But when we go, who knows which shall return,
When growing dangers rise with each new morn?
Farewel, ye little ones, yet tender wives,

For you alone we would conserve our lives!
But cease to mourn, 'tis unavailing pain,
If not fore-doom'd, we soon shall meet again.
But, O ye friends! in case your comrades fall,
Think that on you our deaths for vengeance call;
With uprais'd tommahawkes pursue our blood,
And stain, with hostile streams, the conscious wood,
That pointing enemies may never tell
The boasted place where we, their victims, fell.

Samuel Cole Williams, editor of the 1927 edition, notes that Timberlake could only have learned the substance of the song through an interpreter. Clearly, the translation into heroic couplets is in the mode of "imitation" rather than close or "literal" translation. It's a pity Timberlake felt obliged to put the War Song into heroic couplets, the most popular mode of his day. A more literal (or modest) version would have given us more insight into the original form and content. What we have now is something that might have come from one of Dryden's dramas.

Timberlake, who did not speak Cherokee, did not think it out of place to complain that "both the ideas and verse are loose in the original, and they are set to as loose a music, many composing both tunes and song off hand, according to the occasion." He did, however, admire song tunes taken from "the northern Indians" (Shawnees, probably). They were "extremely pretty, and very like the Scotch".

from A COMPARISON OF PUEBLO AND PIMA MUSICAL STYLES, George Herzog, *Journal of American Folklore*, vol. 49, (1936).

Herzog writes about those "meaningless syllables" I discussed in the Introduction, but does not do much to understand them. A suggestive discussion occurs in "Song in Piman Curing," by Donald M. Bahr and J. Richard Haefer in *Ethnomusicology* (XXII, no. 1, January 1978). The songs, they say, are in *"almost* another language," (p. 119); part of the text, rhythm, and melody that together "lead the patient through a set of riddles on the nature of the dangerous object" that has caused the sickness.

LAGUNA CHAKWENA KACHINA SONG

Herzog doesn't explain how flowers are thrown "down from the sky." Perhaps the children threw the flowers from the rooftops. Compare the Hopi Hevebe song early in this book, where elders pour water onto the girls.

PIMAN FLUTE SONG

This Flute Song of the myth of *na.'sia* ("Flute-Lure") was also used as a love-charm song.

MEDICINE MAN'S SONG

This Pima song, says Herzog, was sung at the end of the cure, proclaiming it a success. The beams of light shining down on the sick person are imaged as corn tassels. The light is a sign of recovery since light symbolizes "power." The problem with this statement, however, as Dr. Haefer has kindly pointed out to me in a letter, is that Pima cures continue throughout one's life, and do not come to an end except at death. (For more on this, see the article in *Ethnomusicology*, noted above. For instance, the authors point out that a patient is not expected to be cured once and for all. "We should think of the cures as having an aspect of initiation *into* a relation with the dangerous object, as well as an aspect of cleansing *from* it." *Piman Shamanism and Staying Sickness*, ed. Bahr et al., University of Arizona Press, 1974, is invaluable on this topic).

SONG FOR GIRL'S PUBERTY RITE

This is the first song from the series sung for the girl's puberty ceremony—it might be pointed out that, as Dr. Haefer wrote me, "perhaps it is unclear from Herzog's article, but based on what we now know, all of these songs are parts of series. The various elements of the series may interact in a number of different ways and it could be said that some of the series would be better expressed in their entirety rather than singling out specific songs. However, that does not bother me about the songs that you have chosen."

RAIN SONG

"Rain song in the rain ritual, with the accompaniment of a notched stick" (Herzog).

CORN SONG

This is the first song of a Pima "Corn Series," sung in the story of Corn, and in ritual. The "low hearts" are pumpkin seeds.

from CEREMONIAL SONGS OF THE CREEK AND YUCHI INDIANS. Frank G. Speck, University of Pennsylvania Museum, Anthropological Publications, vol. I, no. 2 (1909-11).

CRAZY DANCE SONG

This is one of the favorite dances of the Creek. It is called Crazy Dance "because the participants behave like wild people, men and women taking freedom with each other's persons and acting in such a way as to provoke mirth." The songs of the Crazy Dance are usually funny or obscene, which suggests, says Speck, straight-faced, "that in some way there is a connection between the dance and the idea of procreation. In other respects, the movements, motions and accompaniments are similar to the other dances. Licentiousness usually follows after it." Women in this dance pay their partners 25¢!

I have ordered the random, "crazy," phrases of the original—"the sense of the above primitive lyric song is not very clearly expressed in the interlinear translation. The singer changes his tense, mood and voice at random," (Speck).

from ZUNI RITUAL POETRY, Ruth L. Bunzel, Forty-seventh Annual Report of the Bureau of American Ethnology, 1929-30.

"Sayateca's Night Chant" is from the Ha'lako ceremony, "Prayers and Chants of the Priests of the Masked Gods." Prayers, says Bunzel, constitute the heart of Zuni ceremonials, and afford their possessor a source of power. Prayers such as this Night Chant must be formally learned, and are not just picked up. Zuni prayers are highly formalized in content and mode of expression, full of fixed metaphors (compare the Old Norse *kenning*), which are the hallmark of the poetic style.

The Sayateca party of god-impersonators has the most elaborate ritual. I have chosen to concentrate on the end of the Night Chant, where it calls for blessings. In arriving at my version, I have used not only Bunzel's final version, but her transliteration of the text.

Concerning the line about house and heart, Bunzel notes that "an empty house 'has no heart'. The heart of the house is anything which has been used by human beings."

For a thorough discussion of the whole chant, see Andrew O. Wiget's "Sayatasha's Night Chant: A Literary Textual Analysis of a Zuni Ritual Poem," *American Indian Culture and Research Journal*, volume 4, numbers 1 and 2 (1980), 99–140. Wiget also provides a translation of the Chant in its entirety.

from THE PIMA INDIANS, Frank Russell, U.S. Bureau of American Ethnology, 11th. Annual Report, 1889-90.

SONG OF THE SWALLOW
I have used parts vi, vii, and viii of the original song. "Circling Songs" (also called "Basket-beating Songs" because of the nature of their accompaniment), were songs for festivals. They were dance-songs, the dancers moving in circles, male and female alternating.

DATURA SONG
The datura is the native thornapple, Datura Meteloides D.C. These hunting songs were used to bring success. They were also used in cases of sicknesses in which the symptoms were vomiting and dizziness.

FOOTBALL SONG
This song was sung the evening before the day of the foot-race. The race did not just involve running fast. Racers kept a ball the size of a croquet ball (made of mesquite or palo verde wood, or even stone, and covered with creosote gum) constantly in the air, sometimes for over twenty miles. Pimas said that they could run faster with the ball than without!

SONG OF THE BLACK LIZARD
I have used parts iii, iv, and v of this song. Medicine Songs were the largest class of songs. Each ailment had an animal, supernatural or natural agency at work. I couldn't find Black Lizard in Pima mythology, but Elder Brother was a sort of competitor to Earth Doctor, the demiurge who sang and danced the world into existence. When the earth shook and stretched, Earth Doctor made the grey spider which he ordered to spin a web around the unconnected edges of the sky. Thus was earth readied for humans (perhaps the last stanza refers to this act).

Elder Brother seems to take over Earth Doctor's creation, and makes a different kind of order. At one point he made a flood, which the first stanza might refer to.

QUAIL SONG
In Native American tales, it is often impossible to tell where natural and supernatural, animal and deity are being referred to. This song could be an animal vignette. Equally, Coyote could be lurking—"out of the west beneath the toahafs bush the moon gave birth to Coyote and then went down."

BEAR SONG

I have only used part i of this song.

SONG OF THE BLACK TAIL DEER

Russell turns the original transcription "ruins windy" into "houses of magic," without any explanation of his reworking.

WIND SONG

I have used parts v and vi.

PUBERTY SONG

A number of details in these songs are mysterious, and left unexplained by Russell. It seems clear that ritual and religious elements are incorporated, but just what the last stanza refers to, I do not know, nor who "I" is.

from WINTU SONGS, D. Dematracopoulou, *Anthropos*, XXX (1935).

These songs were collected in the summers of 1929/30/31. Dream Songs formed the chief feature of the Dream Dance Cult which was introduced about 1872 and held sway for some forty years. Such songs were given during sleep by a dead friend or relative, and were then performed, along with a dance. They then became common property. In Wintu cosmology, the Land of the Dead is referred to as Above, The West, the mythical Earthlodge of the Flowers, The Milky Way along which spirits travel to their final resting place.

Dematracopoulou notes that the songs exhibit certain set forms, mostly varieties of repetition. I have adapted some of these patterns.

I through VI are Dream Songs. The last two are not.

I   YOU AND I SHALL GO

1929. Sung by Harry Marsh. "This song," Dematracopoulou notes, "is considered to contain an amorous or at best a romantic flavor."

II   MINNOW AND FLOWERS

1929. Anonymous.

III   SLEEP

1929. Anonymous.

IV   DANDELION PUFFS

1929. Sung by the shaman Jim Thomas. "Sways like women while men dance" is my extrapolation of Dematracopoulou's "swaying rhythmically," which translates a word applied to women swaying with bent elbows and forearms pointing upward as accompaniment to the dancing of the men. During the performance of the Dream Dance, men danced in a circle round the fire. The women were drawn up in two lines on either side, swaying and waving flowers and handkerchieves. Dandelions represent spirits which float away, and this song is dedicated to funerals. The celebrants sway, hold the seedheads, and then blow on them all together. Such a ritual probably originated with this song, Jim Thomas' Dream Song.

V   THERE ABOVE

1929. Anonymous.

VI   STRANGE FLOWERS

1929. Sung by Old Alexander.

SONG OF THE PREGNANT WOMAN
1930. Sung by Jennie Curl.
SONG OF THE QUAIL
1931. Sung by Sadie Marsh.

from CREATION MYTHS OF PRIMITIVE AMERICA, Jeremiah Curtin (Boston, 1898).

These are two of the four spirit songs Curtin collected from the Wintu. I have not altered the word order; merely rearranged and shaped.
SONG OF HAU, THE RED FOX
Curtin notes that "the celestial Hau is described as travelling along the Milky Way." Hau puts in only a few appearances in the myths Curtin collected, but he seems a beneficent spirit—he brings the first manzanita berries, for instance. Since the occasion of these songs is the making of new shamans in the sweat-house, and since a whistle was the sign that a spirit has arrived on the housetop, Hau's whistle would seem to have ritual significance.
SONG OF WAIDA WERRIS, THE POLAR STAR
Curtin notes, from the standpoint of a solar mythographer, that "hair, in Indian mythology, as in other mythologies, is the equivalent of rays of light when connected with the sun and with planet luminaries." One might remain sceptical.

NOTES TO ADAPTATIONS FOR THE REVISED EDITION

from MUSIC OF THE ACOMA, ISLETA, COCHITI AND ZUNI PUEBLOS, Frances Densmore, Smithsonian Institution, Bureau of American Ethnology, Bulletin 165 (1957).

BUTTERFLY SONG
Part of "Flower Dance Songs," this song was sung by boys who made new songs each year. Densmore writes that through February and March of each year the Acoma hold a dance "as an invitation to the flowers to bloom again." It is not related to rain or crop ceremonies but is "a simple gathering of the people, beginning at sunrise and ending at sunset." Densmore collected the work in this volume from 1928 to 1940.
SONG TO A BEE
This is from the section "Corn-Grinding Songs," and is "very old." It was sung by the women at Isleta as they ground corn early in the morning. The words for "bee" are "napa" (flower), and "juya'de" (fly). Densmore notes that "there is undoubtedly a poetry in the words which we miss in the translation."(Densmore's translation is "Flower-fly, how pretty you sound./ I am very lonely but you sound too far away.")

from TETON SIOUX MUSIC, Frances Densmore, Smithsonian Institution, Bureau of American Ethnology, Bulletin 61 (1918).

I had overlooked these three songs until I came across them again in Julian Rice's "Hearing the Silence Through Lakota Songs," *Studies in American Indian Literatures*, vol. 8, no. 2 (Spring 1984), pp. 35–39. I probably overlooked them because I hadn't understood the cultural context. Densmore (quoted by Rice) had pointed out that "the melodic feeling in many Chippewa and Sioux songs seems to be for the interval between successive notes while the melodies of the white race are based on 'keys', which are groups of tones having a systematic and definite relation to a keynote." Rice notes that "while the white music always returns to a central 'known' reference point, the Lakota expression becomes music because it celebrates the unknown silence, the interval. The best songs, inspired and composed by spiritual sources and received in dreams, do not allow the formless to be forgotten." And the song "May The Sun Rise," says Rice, celebrates "the miracle of spirit manifesting itself as vision matures." The sun, "or the newly received perceptive power," illuminates a world not previously in existence, and "as the song itself is sung, the earth appears." Of "A Wind Wears Me," Rice notes "the metaphor of a man being worn, of being a garment or form for the spirit to enter, is used repeatedly in Lakota songs," and of "A Rainbow-Hoop Wears Me," he says a physical form conveying the invisible is the hoop carried by an elk dreamer, which is often called a rainbow, because part of the rainbow is visible and part below ground. "The transitory aspect of the rainbow may be thought of as uniting the known and the unknown in a space-time continuum. Again the idea of the vision of this continuum, taking possession of the mind and requiring incarnation, is expressed in a song, 'worn' by the singer, as a spectrum differentiating sacred power so it is comprehensible. The witnesses may undergo spiritual transformation when they behold the singer, a familiar member of the community, played by a sacred power."

from PAWNEE MUSIC, Frances Densmore, Smithsonian Institution, Bureau of American Ethnology, Bulletin 93 (1929).

I confess that I found this song not in Densmore but quoted and discussed in Alexander Lesser's *The Pawnee Ghost Dance Hand Game* (Madison: University of Wisconsin Press, 1978). Lesser notes that "the song embodies the relationship of the Crow and the Moon from which the bird's power comes, and indicates also that the Moon is the night overseer of things on earth, reporting them in the beyond. The Crow is telling the people on earth of the activities in the land of the departed." This song, number 51 in Densmore, was sung by Effie Blane and based on Ghost Dance visions she'd used in the hand game. (The Ghost Dance reached the Pawnee in the 1890s; the old hand game was transformed from a gambling game into a four-day ceremony of cultural renewal, where winning meant being in touch with the controlling influences of the spirit world and was linked to the promise of the Ghost Dance.)

It is helpful to note that Crow and Eagle are the two most important birds in the Ghost Dance, as we can see in the following Sioux Ghost Dance song which Mooney recorded in *The Ghost Dance Religion and the Sioux Outbreak of 1890*. The message of the Ghost Dance's hope (the return of the buffalo and of the dead) is brought by these sacred birds:

> The whole world is coming,
> A nation is coming, a nation is coming,
> The Eagle has brought the message to the tribe.
> The father says so, the father says so.
> Over the whole earth they are coming.
> The buffalo are coming, the buffalo are coming,
> The Crow has brought the message to the tribe,
> The father says so, the father says so.

from ESKIMO TALES AND SONGS, Franz Boas, *Journal of American Folklore*, vol. 7 (1894).

Collected in Cumberland Sound, 1883–84, and "composed by a young man called Utitiaq, who went adrift on the ice while sealing and did not reach shore until after a week of hardship and privation." (In the *6th Annual Report [1884–85]* of the Smithsonian Institution Bureau of Ethnology, Boas includes the music for this song.)

from SONGS OF THE TEWA, Herbert Spinden, *Exposition of Indian Tribal Arts*, New York (1933).

A corn-grinding song. For more on the Tewa, read Alfonso Ortiz's classic *The Tewa World* (Chicago, 1969).

from ZUNI TEXTS, Ruth Bunzel, *American Ethnological Society,* Publication 15 (1933).

This seems something like a comic version of the "Deer Song" tradition, when the hunter seeks to attract the deer. It comes from a story which Bunzel titles "The Lame and the Blind," in which two brothers go on a trip. They decide to catch an antelope, and stop by a hollow tree. With the younger brother shaking his rattle, they sing this song. They sing it four times, until the antelope get the point. "Someone is insulting us," they say, and a large buck rushes over, only to get his foot stuck in a knothole, trapping himself. The younger brother dispatches him.

from PASSAMAQUODDY TEXTS, John Dyneley Prince, Publications of the American Ethnological Society, vol. X (1921).

The Passamaquoddy are an Algonquin-speaking people who live in Maine. Prince notes that a large amount of Passamaquoddy oral literature was in the manuscripts of one Hon. Lewis Mitchell, former Indian member of the Maine legislature. This collection came into Prince's possession, but it was all destroyed by fire in 1911. Mitchell reproduced the work from memory at Prince's request. The reproduced work included this song.

Something about this song makes me suspicious. ("I think you are right to be suspicious," wrote Robert Leavitt, director of the Micmac-Maliseet Institute in response to my queries.) In particular, in the original, "The time has not yet come / when they did not hunt" sounds suspiciously like the nineteenth century's "dying/vanishing Indian" theme. I made my own, linguistically untenable, extrapolation of these two lines. I also omitted line 7, "the road of the great spirit," though I probably should not have. The last line, Leavitt notes, should probably be "This song in the mountains."

The "spirits' road" is the Milky Way (*possesomuwi awt*, "star-road" or "star-path") which Leavitt notes "implies some sort of connection between this world and another, sometimes called the land of the ancestors or the land of the spirit(ual being)s." (Compare Dematracopoulou's Wintu "Six Dream Songs.") The lines about the hunters following the bear refer to the widespread Algonquin legend in which the stars making up the Great Bear constellation are men hunting the bear. The chase begins in spring. In fall, the blood of the wounded bear falls, turning the leaves red. In winter, the hunters succeed in killing the bear, and its fat is the falling snow. Spring melts the fat and turns it to rising sap.

from NAVAJO GAMBLING SONGS, Washington Matthews, *The American Anthropologist*, vol. II (1889).

These are songs from Kestcè, a favorite winter game, to some extent sacred, the object of which is to locate a stone hidden in a moccasin. The songs depend on a legend for their explanation: "Recited by themselves, they seem almost meaningless; sung in connection with the story they are intended to embellish, their significance is at once apparent." The myth tells of the animals gambling to see if it should be permanently day or night; those who saw better at night made up the night-team, and those who saw better by day made up the day-team.

5 : MAGPIE SONG
This is the song Magpie sang at the request of the Wind-god: "Sing a song of morning." It was late, and the animals were all tired, and somewhat indifferent. After this song, all the

animals left for their homes. (Morning's footsteps are, of course, the white markings on Magpie's wings.)

14 : GROUND-SQUIRREL SONG I

As the game progressed with little advantage to either side, the animals turned their attention to composing songs about themselves or their opponents. This is one such song, sung presumably not by the Ground-Squirrel, but by some other animal. Since the next song, "Ground-Squirrel Song II," is, as Matthews notes, "an ironic song sung by the animals in derision of smaller beings who attended the game," perhaps this song is ironic too.

from SONGS OF THE COPPER ESKIMO, Helen H. Roberts and D. Jenness, *Report of the Canadian Arctic Expedition, 1913–18*, vol. XIV (1925).

These songs were recorded on phonograph at Bernard Harbour, in Dolphin and Union Strait, and at settlements nearby, between 1914 and 1916. (This volume contains all the music to the songs.) In the Preface, Jenness says that "Eskimo songs, as a rule, are comprehensible to their composers only; their obscurity, and the limited knowledge of myself and my interpreters, will explain the imperfections, and I fear sometimes the errors, of the translations." The translations are, indeed, not easy to follow, and sometimes downright baffling or even surreal (e.g., "his eyebrows wishing to meet"). It is often hard, given the paucity of notes, to know whether a song is intriguing poetry or simply fragments. At other times, the notes rescue us from what seems to be an insoluble riddle:

> My child when it was about to cry,
> Four eyes though they followed us,
> Their little evacuation over there.

Of this, Jenness notes: "This was said to be the incantation of a polar bear that was pursued by a dog. The 'child' is the bear's cub, and the 'four eyes' are the dog's two eyes, and two white spots, one over each eye, which the bear mistook for another pair of eyes." What the last line means is anybody's guess, though Jenness does note that an alternative line means "we evacuated"!

14 : DANCE SONG

Sung by Uloqcaq, a man from Kiluciktok. Mammoth ivory was found in the Mackenzie Delta and westward. The Native people ascribed it to "a somewhat fabulous monster which they call Kiligvak."

16 : DANCE SONG

Sung by Ciniciaq, a Piuvliq man, and composed by his father.

26 : DANCE SONG

Sung by the old shaman Ilatciaq, from Kiluciktok. Jenness writes of this song: "Its theme changes with the composer's thoughts. First he recalls a winter journey when he was riding on his sled, covered with caribou skins; the wind nearly blew them away, and he attributed this to the maleficence of his enemies who were seeking his death. He passed on to the joy he felt at a certain dance when he taught his audience a new song. Then he remembers a shamanistic performance when his guardian spirit took possession of him and spoke through his person; and he remembers how he avoided looking at his fellow-shaman Kannuva who was holding a seance at the same time. Finally comes a sealing episode. . . . "

The song may proceed through association, but one can detect an organizing theme of taking, giving, receiving. The song ends with something hard-won, between having and not having.

29 : DANCE SONG
Sung by Kanura, a Coppermine River boy.

38 : DANCE SONG
Sung by Hupa, a woman from Piuvliq.

52 : DANCE SONG
Sung by Nijaqtalik, a man from Coppermine River.

53 : DANCE SONG
Sung by Kaneyoq, a Piuvliq girl. Note that a number of these songs are about composing. This one is said to be made up of three separate songs. For helpful comments on the self-conscious process of song composition, see Tom Lowenstein's introduction to his translations of the songs collected by Knud Rasmussen in the 1920s: *Eskimo Poems from Canada and Greenland* (Pittsburg, 1973).

74 : DANCE SONG
Sung by Quayojana, a Coppermine River man. One would like to know the private circumstances of this song, but there are no notes.

123 : DANCE SONG
Sung by two Mackenzie River women, Unalina and Cakaiyoq.

ACQ 0600   3/1/94

ACQ 0600   3/1/94